A MIRACLE TO PROCLAIM

Firsthand Experiences of Healing

A MIRACLE TO PROCLAIM

Firsthand Experiences of Healing

Fr. Ralph A. DiOrio

IMAGE BOOKS
A Division of Doubleday & Company, Inc.
Garden City, New York
1984

Library of Congress Cataloging in Publication Data
Main entry under title:
A Miracle to proclaim.
1. Spiritual healing—Case studies—Addresses, essays, lectures.
2. DiOrio, Ralph A., 1930-   —Addresses, essays, lectures.
I. DiOrio, Ralph A., 1930-
BT732.5.M57 1984   234′.13

This Image Book Original published March 1984
by special arrangement with the Office of the
Apostolate of Prayer for Healing, Worcester, Massachusetts

ISBN: 0-385-19241-X
Library of Congress Catalog Card Number: 83–18218

ACKNOWLEDGMENTS

May the Divine Physician, Jesus Christ,
Son of God, Soulwinner for all mankind,
bless all those who have helped in the
compilation of this book. The Apostolate of
Prayer for Healing and Evangelization expresses
its intense gratitude to Sr. Madeleine Joy, S.P., RN,
for her competent service in not only compiling
the hundreds of cases for file work,
but also in compiling the specific cases
of persons claiming healing, who in turn
have expressed their desire to tell their stories.

DEDICATION

TO THE SICK AND TO THE SUFFERING,
   who are always among us,
we offer our privilege to serve.

May everyone who reads, come to
   the Lord refreshed and restored.
May their hope for the future
   become the faith of the present.

CONTENTS

IF YOU HAVE
MET CHRIST,
GO FORTH
AND PROCLAIM
HIM TO THE
WORLD!

POPE JOHN PAUL II

FOREWORD

An interesting story is related by a worldwide evangelist. A Moslem beggar in Africa—who, because of polio, had crawled on the ground for thirty years, begging—came and was healed in the evangelist's crusade. As he stood on the platform in tears, he cried out, "JESUS CHRIST MUST BE ALIVE! OTHERWISE, HOW COULD HE HAVE HEALED ME? Mohammed is dead, but JESUS LIVES! LOOK AT ME! YOU KNOW ME, I HAVE BEGGED IN YOUR STREETS. NOW I CAN WALK. LOOK AT ME! NOW I CAN WALK. LOOK! THIS JESUS LIVES!"

What greater sermon could be preached than that? What greater witness could be told than that? It was exactly the same kind of incidents that occurred in Chapters 3, 4, and 5 of the Acts of the Apostles. That very truth of Him Who lives and Who has never left His people orphans is a realistic reenactment of the resurrected power of God in this twentieth century.

When a person receives such an extraordinary blessing from God as restoration to health from illness, such a person is set apart by the Divine Provider. He or she is designated to be set apart from humanity; so that being so set apart, he or she may go back to humanity as a recipiently blessed soul, to speak, to witness, and, so doing, to reach many other human beings with the gospel of love and peace.

According to Acts 1:21–26, each recipient of God's supernatural blessings is "bound" that he or she go forth and witness to the resurrection. This witnessing presupposes that he or she who witnesses not only knows *about* Jesus, but that he or she *knows Jesus!*

To every person who witnesses God's activity in his or her life, Jesus holds a status of not just One Who lived and died.

Nor is He just One Whose life we study or read. Jesus is not a historical figure in an "evergreen bestseller." But Jesus is a LIVING PRESENCE!

God usually uses people to help people. God's purpose is soulwinning. Like a cathedral, peace that flows from soulwinning has to be constructed patiently and with unshakable faith. And those called by the Lord to be His hands and His feet, His heart and His mind, His thoughts and His voice, are best gifted to convey their testimony when they themselves, affirmed by God Himself, proclaim that God-experience in a Truth that is founded in authentic roots.

Sometimes God appears to our limited mind as "silent" and "unaware." He may even appear as "uncaring" for us. But then, suddenly, in our most bleak moment, He stirs all our faculties to faith in Him: our hearts, our minds, our bodies, our intellectual and volitional responses to His inspirations. Then these new insights, these new experiences of His providential grace restoring our illnesses flow over us; they are like rivers, streams and brooks. All sorts of divine graces showering upon us God's fresh "baptism of love." In this experience, people so divinely blessed bask in the joy of holy abundance. They do not want to leave this newfound ecstasy. It is Mount Thabor! But, facing the reality of living, they must come down the mountain; and when they do, they must speak, they must tell every man and woman, every human person, that they have met the Lord. He is real! He is alive! The chapters herein are personal lives that somehow have the need *to tell, to speak* of their encounter with a Miracle-God, a God who touched their lives *right here in the present.*

The stories of this book are not only to be read, but should be penetrated to perceive these healing phenomena as a light revealing a presence, the presence of the Invisible God made real through His birth, suffering, death, and resurrection. May each of these narrations be for you a door to the Living Healer.

There can be
no end to
God's power,
it is
inexhaustible.
Let there be
no end to
our faith.

CARDINAL NEWMAN

INTRODUCTION

Everybody loves a story! But when a true story, factual and simple, humble and honest, is told, it necessarily holds an honor as a genuinely good influence. Stories of electrifying incidents of the Almighty upon the human cause the reader to perceive that the supernatural is alive. A true story, moreover, if it be a good one, deserves to be "proclaimed"; indeed, publicly "witnessed"! In the following stories, the persons narrating their encounter with God write their narratives in the first person singular. The stories are so sensitively personal that we the readers should commend these persons for their complying surrender to the Holy Spirit, Who in turn has activated their spirit of "holy boldness." This valorous spirit demonstrates itself with a sense of holy joy, which overcomes the natural timid spirit of "fearfulness." Fearfulness has always been a barrier for humans who plod through life apprehensively, perhaps torturing themselves when it comes to disclosing those sensitive, precious moments or incidents of their lives. Precious, indeed, are those occasions of human and divine interaction coupled gently in the healing hand of a Miracle-God.

The stories herein are of nothing more than grateful human hearts wanting to tell the world that all can be well when one not only recognizes but also turns in faith to a God Who alone can dispense life. Human vulnerability exposes oneself to criticism, even ridicule. Furthermore, it can account for the sum of all psychological fearfulness, that is, being rejected, especially by those uninitiated to a real, positive personal experience of God's genuine presence *alive* in them. In rendering gratitude to the God of all mercy and love, all timid weakness is dispelled. It is replaced by the influx of healing strength, urging and mustering the recipients of holy grace to childlike frankness in communicating their story. Each event necessitates supernatural belief that *God overshadows human lives with positive blessings if human lives would but only let the divine visitor in.*

Such is the theme and purpose of this book. Its pages reveal persons from all walks of life. They are human beings blessed by God. They are human persons who have allowed embarrassment to slip away and to yield to the newborn baptismal strength residing in freedom of truthful disclosure. These are their lives. The Divine Life touches delicately and opportunely the human life experiencing a desperate moment. It is always interesting to read romances as to how "new life" comes to "the old." It is even more exciting to perceive how hope for a better future becomes materialized in and by the presence of faith, transforming the present moment of anguish and pain, fear and danger, into one of healing and restoration.

The true stories told within these pages are authentic episodes of men and women, the young and the old, the poor and the affluent, the professional and the common laborer. All humanity is represented and portrayed, and for this reason it is expected that the book will be one of inspiration and interest to people everywhere. Above all, it will offer hope to anyone who searches the labyrinthine and multiple dilemmas so baffling to life.

We will meet here many people who are now living productive and meaningful lives despite whatever sickness they may have had. Now, through and after their healing, they are walking in the presence of the Almighty *restored, renewed and reborn.* They walk not alone—God is at their side. He dwells alive in their hearts as the resurrected Christ. Their new life exists in Resurrected Power.

To the reader who journeys with the person in the narrative, such a one also can experience the same presence of a living God who offers to touch their own lives through the witnessing experience of another human creature. These first-person accounts serve as an actual grace for the reader to understand HOW BIG GOD REALLY IS! These narrated events, moreover, hold within themselves the power *to spark* into a new living, vital flame a restored human being living mainly in the Holy Spirit of Faith. What they demonstrate so simply is that GOD IS ALIVE IN ONE'S LIFE! These stories have the power to show a befogged humanity—groping amid daily fear and anxiety, searching for absolute truth, that there does exist the love of a *Miracle-Working God!*

As long as we humans traverse the sands of the earth, as long as we are still on this side of eternity, there will always be hope for the future, for a better tomorrow, a better world. When people are sick, when people are close to the portals of eternity—that inevitable absolute reality—they by some natural characteristic, by some innate instinct, *want to live, not die!* And so, when all else has reasonably—and perhaps at times even beyond the reasonable—been rendered, then one *humbly* turns oneself to the gaze and power of the Almighty. In so doing, one desperately searches for true genuine blessing, authentic and valid, from representatives of the loving God dwelling in His Church, among His people. It is interesting to note that people come to services of healing and prayer precisely because of this security and assurance. Certainly they come *not* for the simple ordinary personages apparently blessed by God as His conduits, as His channels of grace. No, the only reason why people come is because of the healing virtue, the healing power of the Holy Spirit dwelling among the contemporary disciples. And no matter how large or small the assembly gathered together may be, the fact remains that God is alive, and the children of God are dependent on this power.

When human lives gather together in the atmosphere of the Holy Spirit, God touches those lives positively. These people will receive God's goodness for them. In every human person some form of faith resides. That faith may be stifled, dusty with years of unuse, perplexed or hazy, perhaps even deliberately turned off. But IT IS THERE! All it awaits is the moment of being hopefully activated through some form of affirmation. People are the same everywhere. They all have the same hunger and response to either personal or en masse evangelism. They yearn for some "Good News."

Great multitudes followed Jesus because they saw the miracles He performed on those who were diseased. Then, once blessed and renewed in some material fashion, their hearts and minds were opened for the preaching of His gospel. Preaching the gospel, with signs and wonders following, gives further proof that we are living not in a dead religion but in Resurrected Power! This was the pattern set forth by Jesus and followed by the early Church. It is also the order of this age, because neither our Lord nor mankind has changed! Our Blessed Lord continues to confirm His word with signs and wonders wherever, according to His directives to the Apostles, His Gospel is proclaimed. Those who believe are blessed; those who are blessed are saved. As each person sojourns the days allotted to his life, if he or she wants what God wants, and if it be wanted for the reason God wants, then, according to an old evangelist, *The Holy Spirit has to be with us and back us up.*

The miracle of healing, whether, in the judgment of human minds, it be "big" or "small," is really to experience God's presence alive in us, and then to witness to others the truth that God intervened with sincere interest in the lives of countless persons. And whether people are either Protestant or Catholic Christians, whether they be pagans who also have the "potential seed" for receiving "sufficient grace" into Christianity's Gospel of Salvation, or be they unchurched, the fact remains that *we all are God's children.* The fact is that our heavenly Father remains "constant," always calling all humanity to Himself.

As sad as it may seem, nevertheless the fact remains that when a person becomes sick, and no further human natural aid is capable to restore him or her, that person looks up to the Divine Power. God is such a genuine and constant lover that He will even take us who have come to Him and have chosen Him as "second-fiddle" lover. In the long run, however, we come to realize that His love is all that counts. We remind ourselves that God created this world. He owns this world. He has a right to run this world. And He has a right to do it through any way He wishes. He will use anything to bring us to Himself: even if He has to use the obstacles we place before Him. But then, that is the love of a true God, a genuine Father.

God will even use sickness and disease, if need be, to bring us to our senses. There is no better time to look up to the heavens than when one is ill, lying upon a bed of pain.

Sickness, with all its symptoms, was introduced to the human race by the author of destruction, Lucifer/Satan, the father and originator of "original sin." But nothing is impossible with God's love and mercy. And the Divine Heart will utilize even those "dismal moments" in life when we think faith is "zero." To visibly speak to us, the Divine Father bestows external manifestations as miracles of His love. In essence, what God is doing is to resurrect, renew, electrify, cause a weakened soul to be personally touched. In so doing, even those who are merely spectators are thrown in for good measure, as they, too, awestricken by the *wonder of it all,* experience *faith in the Person of Jesus Christ, Faith in the Heavenly Father, Faith in the Power of Their Unity: THE HOLY SPIRIT!*

TO CREATE FAITH IN THE PERSON OF JESUS CHRIST! WHAT A REMARKABLE GIFT OF THE FATHER THIS IS! Faith in our Blessed Lord Jesus Christ and in the trustworthiness of His promises is the scope of our ministry. It is the only scope, moreover, for presenting this book. Disease can serve as an occasion to bring us to God's word, God's sacraments, God's life. By preaching through pen or mouth, by factually presenting the Living Presence of God through signs and wonders to the wounded seekers, faith in Jesus and His promises is had. Paul himself tells us that "faith comes from what is preached, and what is preached comes from the word of Christ" (Romans 10:17). Faith is never—and will never be—born of our human sympathy, nor through our human pity. It will never be born through our discussing with people their pains and their aches, their weaknesses and their sicknesses. Faith unto healing is born only when we hear the word of truth, and enter His sacramental life, that life that shed itself so copiously from the wounds He bore while hanging on that Cross.

The stories that are unfolded within this book will be uti-

lized by Almighty God to invite other struggling persons to
the foot of salvation, to God's infinite love and mercy, to His
healing touch. These stories will demonstrate how people do
receive healing. They also disclose the various ways the
healing hand of their God conveys His salvific love. Some
people will be seen as healed through the group prayer of
faith. Some others will be seen as healed by being prayed
over individually. Then others will disclose through their own
narration how they themselves were healed through their
own faith, which came afire and alive while they were bask-
ing in the meditative truths of God's Holy Word presented
from the altar or from platforms. Others will show how the
Lord healed them when He came to them through His sacramental life. How beautiful to be touched by God!

Most important, these testimonies indicate beyond the
shadow of a doubt the objective, ultimate purpose of healing:
THE SPIRITUAL AWAKENING. Without exception, we will
observe a *profound change* in the innermost being of the one
who truly experiences the Divine Healing. This is the spiritual awakening and awareness. This is the absolutely indis-
pensable part of the Divine Healing experience.

The tool that influences the reader is *truthful witnessing*.
These trustworthy narrations have undergone scrutiny and
scientific investigation. Each case narrated will, of necessity,
accent roots founded upon the rock. These are (1) God exists,
(2) God through His son, Jesus, loves us, (3) supernatural
events such as divine holistic healings do occur in our lives,
(4) God constantly offers his miraculous power to heal sick
bodies and spirits, and (5) this power is available to all of us.
The essence of each story, then, is based upon God demon-
strating His active love upon mankind's needs: the *God of
eternity* touching the *human of earth in the now*. Each case
has been scientifically documented, carefully clarified, and
recorded at the office of the Apostolate of Prayer for Healing
and Evangelization by our staff Clinical Directress, Sister
Madeleine Joy, S.P., R.N.

A point of interest to the reader is that many doctors come
to our services. They present themselves either because of
natural curiosity or for the furtherance of holistic medical

concepts pertaining to their professional expertise. Others come because they themselves, being personally rooted in godliness, seek divine prayer for healing either for themselves or for relatives and acquaintances. These professionals witness firsthand many people who experience dramatic (immediate) physical healings, psychological blessings and spiritual restoration. To their astonishment, and sometimes overwhelming observation, they are reassured by the positive change of health in many of their patients who come to them for reexamination. Both to their joy and to ours, many of these professionals later notify our office concerning the changes in their patients as to either definite total healing or to a progressive healing restoration. Some of the stories contained within this book are commented on by such professionals.

The effects of such observation and witnessing are innumerable. The miracle of all healing lies in the realization that millions come to know God through these sensitive personal experiences. Millions express the great hurt that they have undergone from the storms of life. Millions speak gratefully of the loving compassion of God, reaffirming them to the NEW BIRTH. Many medical professionals, men and women, may come to such services with complete ignorance. Some of them enter this strange arena and atmosphere of intense Divine Love with pre-conceived attitudes, with reluctance, or with scientific prejudices. Being scientists and physicians—this being understandable—they may look upon these healing phenomena with skepticism. However, as they sit in the audience, and as they watch the unfolding experiences of intense prayer, faith, love, and forgiveness, they themselves become suddenly transformed in a new vision of golden faith, treasured hope, heart-beating love. Suddenly their humanistic attitude is turned around. With a sparkle in their own eyes at the inexplicable phenomena, they, too, are touched by some supernatural influence to grasp a voice from heaven saying not only to the multitudes, but to them individually, "COME TO ME. HERE IS MY TEACHER, MY SON, JESUS, WORKING AMONG YOU." The entire experience seems to be like a mandate of God. It causes us to stop, to listen and to reevaluate who we are, where we are going and who our God is.

God, being God—and the ways of God are not the ways of man—is electrifying all the observers, taking them from their own journey of doubt to faith, from hope to positive blessing. Suddenly, in this unusual cloud of God's awesome presence, marvels of all sorts burst forth. Events occur, for example children beginning to walk, people hobbling out of wheelchairs, other sickly, burdened people becoming more strengthened and invigorated as they proceed to follow the energizing Divine Power permeating in some strange fashion their weakened humanity. New life flows through them. It is joyful to see how saddened faces suddenly change: eyes begin to sparkle, smiles begin to shine. Smiles and sparkles that for so long had been absent now resurrect and release the inner hurt to the flowing of joyful, happy and grateful tears. Hearing aids are withdrawn as ears begin to "pop" to the sounds of God's creation: people claim hearing. Those who were once deaf and those who were once blind now claim healing emphatically and demonstratively.

The crowds are in awe! They stand in amazement! They raise their hearts as they applaud the experience of happiness and joy returned. Their own tears cause them to raise their whole being to Him who is the Divine Healer. Chanting hymns, all commingle in a prayerful spirit of joy and gratitude to a God Who they may have thought was "way up there," far removed from the weary, broken world of humanity. The new hope, now present, enriches every person in that place with the truth that no matter what the disease may be, ALL THINGS ARE POSSIBLE WITH GOD! The service being concluded after four or five hours, those who attended begin to leave with a sense of having touched heaven—that the sacred spot of God's all-powerful presence has been shared by the Divine Himself with them in a deeper faith. Over and over again, their hearts and minds willingly proclaim the new God-insight that if we poor mortals would only yield our lives completely to God, remarkable things would begin to happen. *This, I believe, is the greatest lesson any human can learn.*

Shakespeare said from the lips of Hamlet that "words

without thoughts never to heaven go." That should tell us that a prayer uttered in simple conversation with God does ascend to His throne. The Lord hears our prayers. He honors them. He opens up new life for us as He responds to our prayers. Without realizing it, we receive somewhere in time that which we have always searched for in the recesses of our soul, namely, the *spiritual impact.* A *spiritual impact* is the real realm of Divine Healing: it is the blessing that enriches us; it is the blessing that unfolds an added dimension to our existence. When a person surrenders to God, God descends upon that person with a tremendous light of the NEW BIRTH. *That glow will always remain. It will share itself with others.* God's spiritual power definitely descends upon us in holy benediction. That benediction is our newfound joy in the Holy Spirit. We become on fire with God's love. HEALED, WE GO FORTH TO TAKE THIS POWER AND TO USE IT FOR THE GLORY OF GOD AND FOR THE SERVICE AND EDIFICATION OF GOD'S PEOPLE!

It is my fervent hope that these chapters may offer healing —that the thoughts expressed by the individuals themselves, who have experienced the power of the Lord through His Holy Spirit, may evoke in the reader the realization of *how important a human person is to God: that persons are not functionaries.* May you, the reader, also be influenced in the deeper values pertaining to the positive absolute realities of life. May the eternal values of Who God is and of who we are never be destroyed by the succession of earthly times and circumstances. May those values that remain always unchanging urge you who read these stories, stories that are so similar to your own, to perceive God's expressive concern for you, too.

May you share with these persons the knowledge that for all of us *the life of all living is that we can be sustained by Him who is life*—sustained in every human, natural foible: brokenness or disease; whether we are tarnished, hurt or dismayed.

The human experience is a voyage of discovery from the womb to the tomb. Death is the key from one state of being into the "eternal next." The journey is filled with hurt and pain as well as with joys and pleasures. But the consolation is that He above journeys that road along with us. He awaits patiently our behest to invite Him in as the two disciples did on their road to Emmaus. If we do so, we will experience Him repairing us, restoring us, even carrying us onward—ever onward! How right was Cardinal Newman when he said, *"There can be no end to God's power; it is inexhaustible. Let there be no end to our faith."*

.

AUTHOR'S NOTE

As of this writing, the following presentations indicate that through both prayer and medicine a positive health change has been recognized. However, as is prudently suggested, any case pertaining to such potentially fatal illnesses as cancer cannot be totally finalized as a complete healing until a five-year period has elapsed.

Daniel Bastian

"TO WALK AGAIN"

Instantly his feet and ankles became firm, he jumped up, stood, and began to walk, and he went with them into the Temple, walking and jumping and praising God.

Acts 3:7–9

This is the story of a seventeen-year-old youngster who had a cancer of the knee bone, medically called osteogenic sarcoma. The characteristics of this illness are that it is highly malignant and the cure rate is disappointingly low. It is among the most common primary bone tumors. These tumors are most common in persons from age ten to twenty. Half of these tumors are situated just above or below the knee, although they may be found in any bone. Surgery is often indicated, along with chemotherapy.

On March 6, 1981, Daniel was hospitalized in Poughkeepsie, New York. His only complaint was a sore leg. X rays showed a mass in the bone above his knee. He had more X rays and a bone scan. Then a biopsy was done on the area where the tumor was seen and the doctors confirmed our worst fears. Dan had a malignant growth known as osteogenic sarcoma.

The next day, we went to Sloan-Kettering Memorial Hospital, in New York City. Another doctor looked at Dan's X rays and bone scan as well as the reports of the doctors in Poughkeepsie. He agreed with their diagnosis and arranged to have chemotherapy started the next day. There was no time to lose.

Dan's experience with chemotherapy could best be described as one long nightmare. Throughout the entire course of treatment he had severe nausea. Many attempts were made to ease the nausea, but they were only minimally effective. In spite of this, part of his treatment included the drinking of large amounts of fluid, and intravenous fluid was administered daily.

In addition to being physically ill from the drugs, Dan was also trying to face the fact that he had cancer. This was a lot to handle for an active fifteen-year-old boy. His world had suddenly been turned upside down. Every day was passed either in a hospital bed or a wheelchair. He spent eleven hours daily receiving treatment in a pediatric day clinic, and at night we went to my other son's apartment, in Queens.

I stayed with Dan constantly in the apartment and the clinic. It was heartbreaking for me, as a mother, to see him so sick and frightened. But he accepted each step that we had to take and never questioned God's will. His faith was strong. He believed that he would get better, although there was no way that the doctor could tell him whether or not they could save his leg. The final decision was to be made in the operating room. I know that he prayed silently and received great comfort in the visits from priests who prayed with him and gave him their blessing. He was the grateful recipient of much prayer in our parish church and throughout the whole county. Many Masses and novenas were offered as people felt that God just had to restore this young boy to full health. The Marist Brothers' Community said novenas that he would have the strength to face his uncertain operation.

Dan survived chemotherapy and it reduced the tumor in his leg to the point where it was possible to operate. In an attempt to save both his leg and his life, the doctor operated, on June 30, 1981, and Dan faced his surgery with courage. Throughout the entire time that he was being operated on in New York City, a prayer service was held for him by the people of St. Mary's Church, in Poughkeepsie.

It was joyous news when the doctor told us that he was able to save Dan's leg! He had removed the bone of his upper leg, as well as his kneecap and part of the bone of his lower leg. He then replaced the bone with a metal prosthesis that was cemented into the existing bones in his upper and lower leg.

My son was hospitalized for a month following surgery. Due to the amount of bone that was lost, the doctors allowed him to do very little. He spent most of the month in bed, eventually progressing to a stretcher and then to a wheelchair, with his leg supported in a straight position. Before leaving the hospital, he was fitted for a full, weight-bearing leg brace. Then he either walked with the support of two crutches and the leg brace or he transported himself in a wheelchair.

We went with Dan to our summer home for the next two weeks, and it was on this vacation that my husband read Father DiOrio's book. Shortly after he read the book, we were offered tickets to see Father DiOrio in Glens Falls, New York. Dan and my husband went with three people who were ill, and they were deeply impressed with the service.

The next day, while driving to the hospital, Dan asked my husband if he felt any sensation during Father DiOrio's service. While my husband had not, my son said that he had felt pins and needles in the leg that had been operated on. At the time, he was back on chemotherapy and was having a blood count every two days. On the Friday prior to going to Glens Falls, his blood count was very low and the doctors had told us that he would probably need a transfusion on Monday. But when he had his count done on Monday it was perfectly normal! Thinking that something was wrong with their new machine, the lab technician repeated the count three times. But, each time, it came back normal. This was most unusual and could not be easily explained.

In September, Dan started going to school on crutches when he was not in New York finishing up his chemotherapy treatments. That same month, Father DiOrio held a healing service in Catskill, New York. A friend mentioned it to us and said that she could get us tickets. So Dan, my daughter, my husband and I went to Catskill early in the morning on September 27, 1981.

As we were waiting outside the church for the woman who was to give us the tickets, one of the ushers approached my husband and offered to bring Dan into the church. My husband told him that we did not have tickets and he responded that it was not important. He proceeded to take my son into the church, and then, at his request, returned and brought me in also. Slowly afterward my husband and daughter joined us.

As we waited for the service to begin, I quietly cried. I was overwhelmed by the beauty and quiet of the prayers in the church and the concern that the usher had for my son even though he did not know him. Most of the next six hours I spent in tears, receiving a marvelous cleansing and release. From then on I knew a deeper understanding of the gift of tears.

When we had previously been called about the tickets that were available in Catskill, the woman had mentioned that there would be a special seating in the front for the very sick and asked if I wanted Dan to sit there. I had thanked her, suggesting that she use the front seating for those who were more seriously ill. At the time, we felt that our son was on his way to a cure. We were attending the service to pray for that special peace that people spoke of.

As it turned out, we were put in the first pew and had the awesome experience of seeing miracles happen before our eyes! Throughout the entire service we marveled at what we saw and heard. We were touched when Father DiOrio came down from the altar and blessed my husband and me.

Toward the end of Mass, Father announced that he would bless as many of the sick as he could. As Dan stood up and put his crutches under his arms for support, Father came right over and brought him into the center aisle. My husband and I stood with tears in our eyes, thanking God for His goodness.

When Father inquired if he was afraid, Dan said that he wasn't. He also said that he believed, and at that point Father took his hands and both crutches dropped to the floor. As Father prayed, my son fell backward, slain in the Spirit. He prayed a while longer, and afterward Dan said that he had felt a warm sensation pass through his leg.

As Dan began to sit up, Father helped him. Then he walked backward a few steps and asked Dan to walk to him. He did it! For the first time in seven months, Dan walked without crutches! He said that he felt fine, and Father asked him to walk from the front to the back of the church. As he did, the entire church came alive in joyful celebration! People were singing, applauding, crying and thanking God. Dan walked back and forth again, and then the pastor asked him to remove his brace. He took it off in the sanctuary and came out carrying it, walking about without help or pain. What a thrilling moment for him and for us! It was one of the most incredible moments of our lives! We were so very grateful to God and happy that Father DiOrio has this special gift through His love.

My son's face just beamed with happiness. The first thing he had said was "Thank you, Father" as he had walked those first steps. Many people embraced him as we left St. Patrick's. Several more wished him well. They were as happy as we were to have witnessed this marvelous display of God's love.

Upon arriving home we called the rest of our family to tell them the wonderful news! The next day we shared with our friends, and Dan went to school without his crutches. I was told by his teachers that he made quite an impression on his schoolmates, although he never did realize this himself. He just quietly walked in, and when anyone asked him where his crutches were he told them about Father DiOrio.

The way that the news traveled in Poughkeepsie was amazing! Many people were overwhelmed and told us that if it had been anyone other than Dan telling the story of what happened, it might have been unbelievable. So perhaps it proved helpful that our family had always been faithful to God and to church. Somehow we seemed to enjoy a good reputation as level-headed people of God, and for this we thank Him.

Seemingly the Lord chose Dan to show His love and to prove that He does answer prayer. People told us that when they heard what happened to him, they believed in God's love and returned to church. On one occasion my son was the crossbearer for the Mass at which a new deacon was giving his first homily. When the congregation saw Dan walking straight and pain-free up the aisle without crutches, tears of thanksgiving could be seen in their eyes. They had prayed for this to happen, and God had answered!

I have noticed that since my son saw Father DiOrio he has a joy and peace in his eyes that was not there before. He knows that he is truly cured of cancer and is not fearful of it recurring. Dan also believes that the others he saw cured were truly more miraculously healed than he was. Although he definitely knows and is deeply grateful that Father's blessing speeded it up, he believes that eventually he would have walked. He is able to discuss what happened to him now and has attempted to help through their treatments others who have cancer. His joy and pleasure in all of the small, everyday things that we so take for granted reflects his special thanks to God.

In October of 1982, a year or so after his healing, Dan was at a school dance. He has always loved to dance, and he fully enjoyed himself. The next day he had pain in his upper thigh. A few days' rest did not relieve it. Finally we called the doctor and had an X ray taken. It showed that the cement holding the prosthesis within the bone had broken away. So the prosthesis was moving within the bone and causing much pain. Dan was hospitalized and had the surgery redone. This time the doctors used a newer and better technique to cement the prosthesis within the bone. While replacing the prosthesis, they also took ten biopsies of various parts of the leg. There was no sign of cancer! In all honesty, while I had been worried about his surgery, I was as certain as Dan that the cancer was completely gone.

After this last surgery, my son saw Father DiOrio again and received his blessing. Father asked him what had happened and why he was on crutches again. Dan told him about going out dancing and breaking the cement in the prosthesis. Father laughed and prayed with him and Dan was again slain in the Spirit.

After the surgery, we had been told that our son would most likely always wear the leg brace. After seeing Father, we took him back for a checkup and once again X rays were taken. The doctor was elated when he saw that the bone was filling in around the prosthesis. He felt that the leg was strong enough and that Dan would no longer need the leg brace!

In this summer of 1983 we are presently on vacation in Florida. Dan has already walked around Disney World for three days. Today he is riding up and down the sand on a rented moped. Isn't this an indication of how completely well he feels? In hearing of the wonderful things that have happened to him, many people have been touched. They seem to be renewed in their own belief in God or in a special Being that they have yet to define for themselves.

PRAYER:
Dear Lord, for so long a time I have hurt in pain beyond description. I hurt and hurt all over, and I hurt again, O Lord. I am so overwhelmed by real pain, and my failure to bear it well has cost me more pain. I hurt all over, Lord. From the very onset of my sickness, O Lord, I have fought against it, against You. I even hid from human solace and treatment. But in the long attempt, all, I was told, would no longer avail my need. And in that last agony of despair, I looked up to You, my Lord, You Who are my beginning and my end. I cried to You with a human cry. You, dear Lord, heard me, received me, blessed me in Your divine mercy. In that pain I came to see Your divine sacrifice. What a pain of Love you bore for me! Our pains united. In that one moment of my surrender, You absorbed my humanity; I opened my eyes, I stood anew. And now, O Lord, grant that I may walk again in the pathways of Your truth.

Christopher Berube

HOPE IN SEARCH OF A
MIRACLE

Be strong, let your heart be bold,
all you who hope in Yahweh!

Psalm 31:24

Desperation has a power within itself to activate inner resources unto positive living faith. Such is the story of Christopher Berube, accompanied with his parents' faith. They were determined never to hear from God a fatal no to their humble but trusting faith. That living faith brought his family from the traumatic shock of an oncoming declared death sentence, from sadness, dejection, fear and anxiety, to excitement and enthusiasm to ripple once again through their home as their child became blessed by a Heavenly Father Who allows all healing to flow from His Risen Son, Jesus.

The case narrated is truly a miracle of Divine Power. Christopher's illness was an inoperable brain tumor that refused to respond to chemotherapy. The medical analysis described the case as a tumor of the third ventricle. The possibility of surgical removal appeared extremely difficult. In fact, it proved impossible. The prognosis was definitely and extremely poor, and without therapy, would prove a hopeless situation.

In spite of this medical conclusion, a mother's love would find a new, proper way to bring hopelessness into positiveness. God would never say no. And so it would be. Divine Providence led Mrs. Berube and her son to the feet of the wounded healer. She attended several healing sessions conducted by the Apostolate of Prayer for Healing and Evangelization. Hope for healing was concluded positively. God received a humble prayer; He respected that mother's broken

heart's intercession. God said YES. Christopher, now seven-
teen, lives in the restoration of a normal life.

The nightmare began on June 29, 1978. My son, Christopher,
was twelve years old then. He fell off of his bicycle and
banged his head, losing consciousness for a few minutes.
When he came to, he was disoriented and had a terrible
headache, something that he had never had before. From that
day on he was constantly plagued by severe and excruciating
headaches.

Two and a half years later, in January of 1981, a neurosurgeon at Children's Hospital, in Boston, Massachusetts, found
a brain tumor the size of a large walnut in the third ventricle
of Chris's brain. The third ventricle is in the center of the
head, and the doctor explained to my husband and me the
extreme difficulty, if not impossibility, of removing a tumor
from this area. He wanted Chris admitted right away because
of dangerous high pressure caused by the tumor.

I was overcome with grief and told the doctor that I
wouldn't allow Chris to be admitted to the hospital, since his
was a hopeless case. Instead, I was going out to find Father
DiOrio. I remember the doctor saying to me, "Who's he? Is he
that guy who makes people pass out?" Through my tears, I
said, "Yes, something like that, and he's going to get Chris
better, because you can't!" Looking at me very sternly, he
told me, "We don't deal with miracles here." I'll never forget
those words, because they crushed me.

My husband and I took Chris and left the hospital. We
spent the rest of that day searching for Father DiOrio, but we
couldn't find him. A wonderful priest on Father's prayer line
prayed with me, but it was not Father DiOrio. The next day, I
admitted my son to Children's Hospital, where they began
grueling and painful testing to pinpoint the exact size and
location of the tumor.

On February 10, 1981, Chris underwent a nine-and-a-half-
hour operation. There were serious complications and he almost bled to death. When the doctor was one fourth of an
inch away from the tumor he had to stop the operation so

Chris wouldn't die. They couldn't get the tumor out. They couldn't even snip a piece of it to see what kind of a tumor they were dealing with.

I saw my son almost die four times within the next few weeks. He got a staph infection, and on March 12, 1981, had to be operated on to remove a bone flap, which is a mass of partially detached tissue used in covering a bone after it has been cut away. His was so badly infected that they had to throw the bone flap away.

Because they were unable to remove the tumor, Chris's cranial pressure was still dangerously high. He had another operation on April 10, 1981, to insert a shunt into his ventricle.

After Chris's first operation, they had begun radiation therapy in the hope that it would destroy the tumor. The radiation therapy made him feel very sick. Later on, he had three CAT scans, and each one of these X rays showed that there was no change in the size of the tumor.

Throughout this whole ordeal, my husband and I began to bring Christopher to Father DiOrio's healing services. We went to every one that we could possibly get to. It was about this time that our son made his Confirmation. My husband and I prayed that God would spare Chris's life as he spared the life of Abraham's son Isaac. We asked Christopher to take the name Isaac at his Confirmation. So our Christopher Eric Isaac Berube was confirmed, and although we didn't know it then, our all-powerful God, in His loving mercy, did spare his life!

At one of the healing services that I attended, Father DiOrio offered the suggestion that, prior to coming to a service, a good preparation might be to make a novena. So, on July 18, 1981, my husband, Christopher and myself began a novena to good St. Anne at St. Anne's Shrine, in Fall River, Massachusetts. This particular novena is said at the shrine for nine consecutive days, ending with a candlelight procession on the feast of St. Anne.

On July 25, the day before the feast of St. Anne and the eighth day of the novena, Father DiOrio held a healing service in Worcester, Massachusetts. My family and I decided to go to the healing service and say our novena prayers there.

At one point during the services that day, Father DiOrio told everyone to pray silently to God as he quietly prayed. We were in the balcony quite far away from him. I had a little cross that had been given to me when I entered the auditorium. While everyone was praying quietly I put my arm around my son and began to place this cross that had been blessed by Father on Chris's head. As I asked Jesus to please cure him, the cross flew out of my hand and appeared to weld itself to my son's head. At the same time, he went flying backward just as though a giant had picked him up and thrown him. It happened with such power that the arm that I had around him nearly broke off. Chris was slain in the Spirit, and although he had experienced this many times before, I knew that this time there was a difference. I just knew that he was being healed!

When my son awakened, he said that the pain in his head was excruciating. This was unusual, as he did not have pain prior to being slain in the Spirit. "It feels like the middle of my head blew up," he told us. The center of his head was the exact location of his tumor.

Chris's condition showed constant improvement following our attendance at the healing service of July 25, 1981. His brain tumor not only stopped growing, but entirely disappeared. The last three CAT scans that were taken showed no evidence at all of a tumor. We thank the Lord for Chris's healing, and good St. Anne, who interceded in his behalf.

PRAYER:
O my God, how can I ever thank You enough. Hopelessness was determined by human forces. But Your divine invitation to faith burst my anxiety and despair from a Good Friday death sentence to the victory of a Resurrected Power. My son, once at death's door, now lives! Oh, how can I thank You for giving me my son back. What a privilege I have to be a mother: to nourish and care for the life that came from my very veins, from my very flesh. What a precious gift life is! You gave him back to me as I gave him to You in illness. I now return love for love as I, like Your holy mother, give my

Christopher to You in holy dedication. Take him renewed, guide him all through the days of his life. Let him use the gift of new life, the gift of new days to spend, as stepping-stones to know You, to love You, and to serve You.

Barbara Bruchon

———◆———

SINCE THAT BLESSED EVENT

Bear with one another; forgive each other as soon as a quarrel begins. The Lord has forgiven you; now you must do the same.

Colossians 3:13

An interesting insight in the healing ministry is that when we pray for the alleviation of a symptom, we must go beneath that symptom to the ultimate cause of the problem. We must consider basic causes of sickness when we pray for illnesses. Some sicknesses return because the entire healing process was not properly completed. This is of the essence of inner healing. In the following narration, done in the first person by Mrs. Barbara Bruchon, the above factors are factualized into a beautiful renewal of a soul steeped in anger, freed by prayer, loved again by a love that never betrays, healed by the touch of a forgiving God.

Since May 13, 1982, I have become an entirely different person. Upon my arrival that day at the Charlotte Coliseum, I must admit that my faith was no larger than a mustard seed. In fact, it would have been difficult to convince me that God existed, let alone that He cared about me as an individual.

Previously I had been hospitalized because of having homicidal and suicidal tendencies. I experienced tremendous rage toward my husband and myself, and the hospitalization did nothing whatever to dispel it. All I did was "play it cool" and my doctor released me.

Hatred consumed me to the point that I did not care about the needs of my three children. I was so depressed that the thought of living from one hour to the next was a struggle. I told my husband that I would kill him, and in bed at night I would plan how his execution and my own could be carried out. It saddens me to think of what my poor children went through and how they stuck by me through it all.

My mother told me that Father DiOrio was going to be in Charlotte, and having seen him on "That's Incredible," I decided to go with my son and a friend. All of my life I had been deeply involved in the occult, and at my friend's suggestion I followed steps to renounce evil. But I became worse, rather than better. So I decided that after seeing Father in Charlotte I would get my estate in order and take my life, but my doctor threatened to have me committed. In a last-ditch effort to forestall me, he called and made me promise from one hour to the next that I would not harm myself. Then I finally took my medication and managed to "float" through the next two days until we went to Charlotte.

While awaiting Father DiOrio's arrival in the auditorium in Charlotte, feeling that I must be among a bunch of Bible-thumping Baptists, I was totally turned off by the whole scene. I kept feeling a penetrating heat flow through my neck and head. It was a little uncomfortable, and I didn't really know that it was connected to anything spiritual. The scent of gardenias was noticeable to me too, but those around me denied wearing perfume.

When Father DiOrio came onto the stage and the Holy Spirit began working through him, I was awestruck. Still, despite apparent "marvels," I was not totally convinced. I thought that it must be a setup; if, by chance, it wasn't, the Lord was going to "blow it" with me if my son was not cured of diabetes. He was not called forward to claim his healing. I was called. Although prior to that day I had never heard of emotional or spiritual healing, since than I have not ceased to praise the Lord.

From the time of that event I have been neither homicidal nor suicidal. I have managed to go back to college and complete the earning of my degree. I also was able to secure a job to support myself and my children while in school. Recently, I was accepted into a masters program in education.

I wrote to my ex-husband and told him of my coming to the

Lord. Then I asked him to forgive me for the bitterness, resentment and hatred that I had felt toward him. Although I made it known to him that I would not divorce him, he later wrote me a curt note and divorced me. At times I still feel bitter about that, but when I do, I ask God to bless him and his new wife.

Two of my children have given their lives to the Lord along with me, and we have been taken care of by Him. David is still diabetic, but his insulin has been cut back. I was always a reserved person, but now I find myself reaching out to others and wanting them to come to the Lord. I really did not care much about people, because it is in getting close to them that you get hurt. But that is all different. My psychiatrist was amazed at the change in me. He has since released me to the Lord!

PRAYER:
"Father, forgive them, for they know not what they do." is a sentence that keeps passing through my mind, dear Saviour. Through my own healing, dear Jesus, I have come to know the power of being released, unbound. By unbinding another, I have come to be free. Thank You, dear Lord.

Sister Francesca Cloutier

———

A DOUBTFUL HEART
CANNOT STAND BEFORE
THE VISION OF THE LORD

*When the disciples said, "We have seen the Lord,"
he answered, "Unless I see the holes that the nails
made in his hands and can put my finger into the holes
they made, and unless I can put my hand into his side,
I refuse to believe."*

John 20:25

This is a nun's story: sensitive of person, gentle of character, warm of concern, but one who, in spite of her struggling perseverance, found it difficult to believe that a great God above could touch human life in the real struggles of earthly pain, including her very own. How did God speak to her? How did He change her doubts into living faith? How did He speak to her in her pain? The answer is quite simple. And it is one that adds new insight into the glory of the Cross, with its rays of triumph. That answer speaks to all humanity from every page of the recorded Gospels and Epistles. It is the echoed theme of human heritage portrayed in speech and song, in prayer and praise, in preaching and in reflection: God sent His Son, Jesus, to the cross to suffer and die because the love of a faithful God would prove that without faith there can never be any hope.

In the weeks preceding Father Ralph DiOrio's visit to our parish, I had no intention of attending his mission. I was a skeptical nun. "You won't catch me in that church," I told Father Mike, our parish priest. Then I called the rectory to order tickets for the sisters who wanted to go, and Monsignor assured me that they would be welcome without them. Thank God that we did not need tickets. If we had needed them I would not have experienced the great love and healing that God had in mind for me. He works in such mysterious ways.

On March 1, 1983, the first evening of the mission, a friend who was going to the church with her family called to invite me to go along for moral support. As they had been like a second family to me over the past eight years, I felt that I could not refuse them this favor. So I went along and, once in the church, was overtaken by the hurts and pain of so many. I spent the next three and a half hours praying for people who were ill, both those who were present and those who were not.

The next night, I went to the home of another friend, who is a hairdresser. On many other occasions I had stayed until late in the evening. But this time I did not. I just wanted to be back in that church to pray for people who were hurting. So I had my hair cut and returned immediately to the church. It was a beautiful evening of prayer and healing and I was just overwhelmed with joy!

The following afternoon I went to the convent and Father DiOrio was having lunch. In the course of our conversation he learned of my physical ailments and told me that I needed a "package deal." Sometime previously I had injured my shoulder. It had required surgery, and after the operation, when the bone had regrown, spurs had developed, shredding tendons on my shoulder. This had caused me to need surgery again, and I was operated on for the second time in January of 1983. In March my arm was still weak and my range of motion was poor. So Father inquired if I would be willing to come up to the front of the church if he called me for a healing that evening. Although I felt that there were many people in greater need of God's healing, I agreed that I would. After all, if it was God's will, then I wanted my shoulder to be healed. But, more than for myself, I wanted it for the faith of those who had encouraged me to attend.

At dinner with friends that evening, the topic of conversation was the mission. Then, rather than remain afterward to use their whirlpool for my shoulder, I excused myself to go back to the church. I was a nervous wreck! But the service came and went and nothing unusual happened to me. Several times I told Jesus: "If that's the way that You want it, it's okay." Actually, my shoulder was secondary to my concern for so many sick people, and I knew that with six months of therapy it would be fine.

When the service was over, Father Ralph sent for me to change the time that he would say Mass the next day. Jokingly, I said to him: "I thought that you were going to call me for a healing of my shoulder!" "That's right," he said. "I'll do it right now." "Please don't do that to me," I said. "I'm frightened!" Within our view were both skeptics and ushers who were still in awe. Although I knew many of them, I was well aware that it was not their presence that frightened me. I was afraid because I knew that deep down in my heart there was still some unbelief. Then Father simply took me by the shoulder and said: "Sister, Jesus wants to use you right now. Please be quiet and let me pray over you." How could I say no to God? So I let Father pray over me, and although I had decided that no one would ever make me keel over, I was slain in the Spirit. It all happened so fast, and I remember thinking that I hadn't given Father a chance to pray. At one point I opened an eye and saw that he was still praying over me. "How are you doing?" he asked. I responded with a mumble and heard him direct me to close my eyes and enjoy it. Christ had evidently taken over my pride, and for a few moments I was oblivious to my surroundings. Pain rushed throughout my body. In fact, I thought that my chest would actually rupture. When I came to, Father Ralph was gone. But God, in His goodness, had seen to it that Father Mike was nearby. Just as the Good Shepherd held His lost sheep, he held me gently as I cried and cried. That night I received inner healing as God relieved me of hurts that were in my heart. Being sensitive to others, I had carried their pain with me and hurt for them. God also freed me of several of my hangups. I was not at all embarrassed upon arising, as ordinarily I would have been. In fact, I found myself ready to proclaim Christ without worrying about what anyone thought.

The morning before Father Ralph left, I asked a parent to substitute for me so that I could attend his private Mass. When he anointed those who wished to be blessed, I was again slain in the Spirit. He finished blessing the others and then knelt on the floor next to me. I felt his hand on my shoulder as he prayed, and all that I could visualize was Christ healing the sick. When I got up I was "radiant" and my shoulder was healed!

The next week, when I saw my physical therapist to have my shoulder checked out, he found that I had regained full range of motion. It was less than two months, and I had been told that it would take from six to eight months, and even then my recovery was not expected to be complete. My therapist also found a new strength in my arm and said that I no longer needed treatments. Then my surgeon told me that only a miracle could have healed it so quickly!

How can I ever thank God enough for His tender mercy and great kindness to me? In His everlasting love, He healed my shoulder. But even more important, He healed my unbelief!

PRAYER:
My dear Lord, my everlasting faithful God, You have not abandoned me; You have touched the loyalty of my dedication with the assurance of Your concern for me. I thank You, Lord, for taking my hope with its future aspirations and molding it into the precious gift of faith for the present.

My Father in Heaven, mere words cannot express the inner peace You have secured me with. All the fear and the uncertainty which weighed upon me in illness, when the familiar and the taken-for-granted comfortableness in our lives is taken from our human grasp, has been healed. In gratitude, I, now blessed by You, pray for others whom You are constantly calling to Yourself as You did me.

Jennifer Corbett

———————

ARTHRITIS HAS NO CLAIM

He is like a shepherd feeding his flock,
gathering lambs in his arms,
holding them against his breast
and leading to their rest the mother ewes.

Isaiah 40:11

Parents know one truth about God and their children. From the moment of conception, a child belongs to God. The child is His. When children are given to us, God does so by sharing them with us through life and through gift. True parents appreciate God's blessing of the earthly trinity, the family, in their marriage. In feeding, clothing, sheltering, the tender hands of mother and father caress their little one's body with love while their gentle words speak lovingly. The tremendous marvel of being channels of God's expressive human life expands into further degrees of love, and of values. As love develops in each moment of time, so do the pains of growing disclose the "other moments," of pain and sorrow: that the child will inevitably undergo sickness or injury.

And so is the case of Jennifer Corbett, age eight at the moment of her healing, March 9, 1980. Little Jennifer suffered the pains and anguish of juvenile rheumatoid arthritis. The cause of this illness is unknown. Although the medical profession, in its expertise, did all that they could, yet little Jennifer ultimately failed to respond to medication. The pain intensified, and even inflamed her hips and other joints. All treatment was determined to be futile. Both parents, in desperation, but with hope in the God Who gifted them with a child's life, approached the Lord's healing altar of love. The Risen Lord empowered her crippled body. Jennifer now amazingly enjoys the gift and the life of liberty to move and freedom to be.

For about five years, Jennifer suffered with juvenile rheumatoid arthritis, a disease that is characterized by episodes of joint pain, fatigue, listlessness and many other symptoms. It all began when our daughter was three and a half years old. The joints that were most severely affected were her hips. During flare-ups she would appear pale and very tired. Many days she was unable to get up and be with the rest of the family, as it was so uncomfortable for her to walk. When in remission, however, she was a bright, happy and active little girl.

The treatment of choice for juvenile rheumatoid arthritis is high doses of aspirin. But even when taking very low doses, aspirin caused Jennifer to become quite ill with liver complications. Most of the other medications for arthritis were either not approved for use with children or still experimental. Over the years, my husband and I took her to several specialists. Throughout this time she was placed on a variety of medications, treated with physical therapy and finally given crutches. Then, at eight years of age, she reached a point of no longer responding to treatment. She had been in acute flare-up for five months and was in too much pain to walk without crutches. Although on the maximum dosage, the medication that she was taking did not help her. The doctor wanted to put her on a drug that had many serious side effects. My husband is a pharmacist and I am a nurse. Needless to say, we were very concerned about the use of this drug but could not see an alternative.

Around this time a co-worker of mine at the hospital where I was employed suggested that I bring Jennifer to a healing service conducted by Father DiOrio. I had attended one of his services in the past but had sat in the lower church and watched it on videotape. Although I was impressed with his charisma, compassion and sincerity, when it came to the actual healings I was skeptical. Being a nurse, I kept looking for a physical explanation. However, I continued to be curious about it. My husband accepted it on faith without the reservations that I held.

So when it was suggested that I bring Jennifer I became very excited about it. According to the schedule, there was to be a service on March 9, 1980, at Sacred Heart Church, in Hopedale, Massachusetts, a small town about ten miles from our home. When the day arrived, my husband was away on business, so Jennifer and I went to the service, leaving the other four children with relatives.

As we were driving to the church, I prayed, "Lord, if anything is supposed to happen to Jennifer today, please let us get a good seat." When we arrived there, the parking lot was filled with cars and buses from as far away as New York. A friend of mine who was directing traffic told me that we probably would not get in. Jennifer was terribly disappointed when she heard this, but we did not give up. The two of us entered the church through a side door. The church was already full and many people were standing. As Jennifer had been on crutches for the past five months, I knew that she would not be able to stand. We were about ready to leave when an usher tapped me on the shoulder and said to come with him to the first row, which had been reserved for handicapped children. At that moment I knew that the Lord had heard my prayer and that this would be a special day for Jennifer.

As the service began we were enveloped with a sense of warmth and joy. Then, a little later on in the service, Father came up to Jennifer and called her into the aisle with him. He wanted to know her name and what her problem was. He then asked her if she knew that Jesus loved her, and she answered that she did. Father carried her to the altar and prayed with her. He then stood her up and told her to run around the altar three times. She did! For the first time in six months she ran! He had her run up and down the aisle. By this time people were crying, shouting and praising God! It was a completely overwhelming experience to actually see my daughter restored to health. I truly knew what it meant to feel the presence of the Lord.

When we left the church, Jennifer was walking without crutches. All of the way home I kept asking her if she was still all right. I was almost afraid to believe that it would last, but she reassured me that she was fine. Our little girl was very excited about going home to see everybody. She could now ride a bike again!

When we arrived home, Jennifer's brother, sisters, grandparents, aunt and uncle were all there to greet her. At first there was a stunned silence, followed by tears of joy, praise and thanksgiving. Then we called her father, in New Orleans, to tell him the good news. We were all so thankful that the Lord had restored our child to good health. Two weeks later, when we returned to the doctor, her physical exam and blood tests were all normal. We told him what had happened and he smiled, saying that he was delighted that she was so well.

It has been nearly three and a half years since her healing, and Jennifer has not had any recurrence of arthritis. She is now a very active and happy eleven-year-old girl. She has many friends, a paper route, takes dancing and piano lessons, swims and rides her bike. Last year she completed an eighteen-mile course in a bike marathon for the benefit of St. Jude's Hospital.

Jennifer is an unusually devout child. She says a rosary nearly every night and makes novenas to Saint Theresa for other people's problems and intentions. Many times her prayers are answered in a noticeable manner.

We believe that the Lord has touched our daughter in a very special way. The one thing that she has some difficulty accepting is why she was chosen when there were many others worse than she in the church that day. Most likely, we will never know that answer. But as time has passed and hundreds of people have been moved in hearing the story of Jennifer's healing, we have come to believe that it was not just a single event for her.

PRAYER:
Dear Lord, I am only a parent. You blessed us with your marriage bond. A child came forth from the seed of honest love. Oh, how happy we were, how happy were our hearts with the new life that came from our own beings. To share with you the grace of bringing a child into this world, what a privilege!

But, one day, dear Lord, suffering came to our child through the decaying pain of juvenile rheumatoid arthritis. How our hearts and minds ached! We would give our own lives to release that foul illness. Oh, God, what a price we mortals must pay for that first sin of mankind. We suffer the effects of original evil. On what could we depend to bear this anguish observed in our little Jennifer? But You were there always in our lives, in our marriage. You gave Jennifer to us. She is Your gift of life. THAT WAS IT! You are a God of life! You are a God of gift! Gift and life go together from You. And so we turned to You, that You might renew afresh and restore the life of Jennifer that You gave us as gift. We prayed! We fasted! We humbly went to Your visible channel of grace. We sought healing for our child. You, dear Lord, heard and accepted an unselfish cry of two parents. You blessed our home again with the healing love for our child. Thank You, Lord.

Nancy Corr

———————

WHAT KIND OF PERSON
DOES THE LORD HEAL?

Lord, I am not worthy. Just say the word, and I shall be healed.

> *Roman Ritual: former Latin Mass: Communion prayer*

What kind of person does the Lord heal? Is this not a question humble people ask? Nobody ever thinks he is worthy of God's blessings—although all of us would want God to bless us. Yes, each and every one of us feels this way. How can one find that answer? The response is very close to us; in fact it is so close that we cannot detect it. The answer is in our fallen human nature. God created you and me. God called you and me to Himself. This is God's world, and God runs it with priority concern for you and me. Sin has taken us away from our salvation. But God sent his Son to earth, according to St. John's chapter 3, verse 16, that whoever would believe in Him would not perish, but find his eternal destiny. Sin interfered with our destiny; it brought its particular characteristic, destruction, to each of us. In so doing, it introduced the "stepping-stones" to death; it inflicted us mortals with illness and disease. But as Chesterton would point out in his dialogues concerning his character Mr. Pond, ". . . the gift of finding fault should be balanced by the gift of finding value." The real splendor of Divine Healing is that God does not just touch the body, He touches the soul. What a reality that is: the human soul! In the case of Nancy Corr, she asked that question concerning whom God should heal. None of us is really worthy of any healing; but the fact remains that God does heal us, because He loves us just as we are. In Him all our humanity is absorbed; in His word, all our human frailty is reformed; in Him, each one of us is healed by His divine love and mercy. To Him, there is no distinction of person: no race, no denominational difference, no status of life. Each of us is His child. If we would just go to Him and recognize Him to be the Father of our lives, we, like Nancy Corr, would find the answer she did: that God came to this earth in the visible form of his Son, Jesus. This Son of God was a prophet, a great teacher and a healer. He fulfilled this mission not just by dying on a cross, but by being raised from the dead. He became the Saviour of the world. To believe in these facts is the message of faith in the person of Jesus, and in this is our healing. *Nancy Corr, through her own struggle, through her own search for healing, finally found Jesus to be her healer. And in so doing, she came to realize that God heals, and helps his people realize that each person is unique and valuable to God—that each person has an important role to play in God's plan; above all, that each person has a divine destiny to fulfill. And as you read this introduction, and as you read the story of Nancy Corr, may something happen today to you that will cause you to realize that God loves you, since He sent His Son to you—because* you have value.

In August 1979, I went to a family friend who was a travel agent to pick up my tickets for Lourdes, France. Pat Lynch was handing me my tickets for my third trip to Lourdes.

Pat said, "Did you ever think of going to the Healing Priest, in Massachusetts?" I replied, "You are the fourth person who has said that to me, but no one ever gives me any information about Father's whereabouts. Just give me my tickets and let me go to Lourdes." I needed Lourdes as I had never needed it before. Pat opened his desk drawer stating he knew the Irish Franciscan brother who ran the buses from the Bronx to the Healing Priest and took out Brother Laurence Grimes's phone number. He advised me to call Brother Grimes when I returned from Lourdes. Upon my arrival home, my mother asked if I had picked up my tickets for Lourdes and I stated I had not only picked up my tickets for Lourdes but I also had information about the bus that goes from the Bronx to the Healing Priest. Although I had promised my mother I would not return to Lourdes without taking my nephew, my own disability had worsened and I was unable to take him. It would have been an imposition, due to my braces and his behavioral problem. But I assured her that I would be on the first bus going to Massachusetts after I returned from Lourdes.

The day I was leaving for Lourdes, as I came out a doorway, three children on bicycles were coming around a corner. They did not see me and as I stepped out, one of their bicycles stopped on my right ankle, throwing me against a wall. But I did not fall.

My brother, Tommy, came to drive me to the airport and I showed him my bruised ankle, which was now swollen. He said he should be bringing me to the hospital for X rays, not to the airport. I told him not to worry, we did not have time for a hospital visit, and I might be the only one who ever went to Lourdes for X rays! I was able to secure ice packs for my ankle on the flight to Paris, and changed airports and planes in Paris, checking my suitcases into long-term baggage as I could not carry any weight.

Once checked in for my flight, I sat down and fell asleep, only to be awakened by an excited French lady who kept pointing to my cervical braces and saying, "De Lourdes, de Lourdes," while taking my hand and indicating a door. It was apparent she had left the plane to get me. She also placed me on the bus from the Lourdes Airport and made the bus driver stop the bus outside of the hotel and insisted he stay with me until the hotel owner acknowledged he had room for me.

It was the first time I was in Lourdes by myself and I was in an area very far from the Grotto. Just being in Lourdes was such a great joy, and I was filled with so much peace! The smiles on the faces of the sick from all over the world remain forever in my heart. Our Lady Treasury of Graces truly gives so many graces to all who come to her, purifying our requests to her Son Jesus Christ, who presents them to God the Father, sending the Holy Spirit as the Healer. My energy level dwindled and my ankle hurt so much I could hardly walk. I could wear only slippers. I was sicker than I had ever been and never got to the healing baths of Lourdes. I had a letter from my doctor that would have allowed me immediate entry into the baths, but I could not raise my energy level enough to get there until the third day. When I finally got there, the baths had just closed for the day. Why had Our Lady allowed me to travel all this way and not allowed me to bathe in the healing water of Lourdes? I could not understand.

I decided not to return to my hotel. I would go for lunch at the Little Flower Tea Shop, where the Irish gather for tea and where I would hear English spoken. While having a pot of tea, a conversation started with three Irish pilgrims, who were somewhat shocked that I was alone in braces in Lourdes. We shared what our visits to Lourdes meant to each of us, before we parted. One man, by the name of Joe, removed his green scapular and, placing it in my hand, stated that he hoped it would bring as much happiness to me as it had to him.

Lightened in heart, I took off for the afternoon blessing of the sick with the Blessed Eucharist procession. At the candlelight procession that evening, in which I was unable to walk, my newfound Irish pilgrim friends warmly greeted me and walked for me as proxy.

The next morning was my final day in Lourdes, as I had a 1:00 P.M. flight to Paris via Ireland on my way home. I packed early and went to the Grotto, attended Mass there and returned through the square. I was halfway to the hotel when I decided to go back to the Grotto once more. As I passed the Crowned Virgin in the square, I asked her to open my heart to say farewell to Our Lady at the Grotto, for she knew I could never return, as I was the worst I had ever been in Lourdes. My disability had increased so much that I knew I would never be able to return. My heart was deeply disturbed by this realization, and I asked Our Lady, if she really wanted me ever to return to Lourdes, to show me a sign within thirty days. My heart was very heavy as I rode to the airport. Arriving early for my flight, I pondered the beauty of the mountains and how Lourdes was part of me.

Once back home, I waited for four days for Brother Laurence Grimes to return to New York. I inquired of him the first bus that would be going to the Healing Priest. I was shocked when he asked, "Which priest?" I just could not believe that there was more than one.

He said, "Father DiOrio?"

I said, "That is the one!"

Brother said that he had a bus going Thursday, September 27. I asked if children were allowed on the bus, because I had a nine-year-old nephew to come with me. "That's all right if he is good," he said, "because there are sick people on the bus and I would not want them disturbed." I told him my nephew had a behavioral problem and I could not vouch for his behavior on the bus. Brother Laurence told me he would leave the decision up to me if I should bring him.

I ordered five seats, and on Thursday morning, my nephew, three neighbors and myself began the bus journey to the Healing Priest. My mother prayed unendingly that no problem would occur because my nephew had to be wakened so early and that he would get dressed and go on the bus without incident. We arrived at Brother Laurence's bus and took the last seat, with the surrounding seats ahead and across for my neighbors, who would understand should any problem arise. We played cards, Monopoly, etc., as Brother Laurence prayed the rosary and explained what would happen that day. I did not hear a word, because my nephew spoke through the entire rosary and prayers. After prayers, Brother Laurence proceeded down the aisle, talking to each person, and when he came to our seat he said to me, "Oh, my dear, you do have a problem." He was referring to the cervical brace I was wearing, which was very evident. "No, Brother," I replied, "I just came back from Lourdes; today is my nephew's day!" I then proceeded to explain my nephew's problem.

Brother Laurence spoke to him a few minutes. But then he asked me what was wrong with me, and once again I explained my nephew needed prayers. Brother Laurence proceeded onward back up the bus aisle to talk to my neighbors and for the third time returned to ask what was wrong with me. The third time I tried to understand why he was not listening to what I was saying and again talked only about my nephew and asked for prayers for him. Finally Brother asked, "Would you remove your brace if Father asked you?"

I answered, "I would if I was healed."

We arrived at St. John's Roman Catholic Church, in Worcester, Massachusetts, at 10:00 A.M. The healing service began at 12:00 noon. Everybody rushed for seats. My nephew and I got the last seats in the last row in the balcony on the right side. It was a lovely New England church, the first I ever saw with four rows of seats in the balcony on each side. After we settled in our seats, my nephew wanted to eat, look around, etc., do anything but not be in church. One of my friends took him for a walk several times. My nephew wanted me to go with him for ice cream. To avoid any upsetting disturbances I went reluctantly, though our seats were being guarded by our neighbors.

Shortly before noon, one neighbor was excited as she explained she was standing on line and a man was telling his healing story. He returned on his first anniversary to thank God for his healing. It did not seem important to me what he was healed from, but I was curious as to what he looked like, what kind of a person he was. I just wanted to know what kind of a person the Lord healed. My neighbor did not think those questions were appropriate to ask. I had been three times in Lourdes and never saw anyone or talked to anyone who was healed. I was so pleased she had talked with someone who was healed.

The music started and everyone was encouraged to sing along. They were singing songs I never heard before, as I had never been to a healing service or prayer meeting. It became quite hot and I was wondering why anyone would close the huge windows behind me. But every time I checked to see why the windows were closed I noted that they were open. I did not understand this "heat" experience. Whenever my nephew spoke, there was a lovely breeze and the heat stopped! My nephew wanted to know when it was going to end, but it had not even started.

Father DiOrio starting talking and praying, and my nephew grew disturbed. I took him by the hand down to the edge of the balcony and made him sit on the kneeler with his arms over the railing. He was pleased that he could see everything. I returned to the last-row seat and, due to my brace, I could see only the other balcony. I could see only straight ahead unless I turned my entire body right or left. From our section of the balcony I could not see the altar. I assumed Father was speaking from a pulpit. He prayed and asked everyone to repeat after him many prayers. He called many people to come to the altar with the sickness he mentioned, each time stating a man or woman and the name of a sickness. He read Scriptures and preached. I was so touched by his teachings and leading everyone in laughter and prayer!

About an hour after the service started, he said he wanted everyone to forget themselves and for what reason they had come, and he led us in prayer for each other. He explained how much Jesus truly loved us and wanted us to be whole. He identified many sicknesses and called some to come forward. I begged Jesus with all my heart to heal my nephew. I could not see Father, but everyone was clapping and thanking Jesus with Father in prayer and song. Every time my nephew would walk up to me and talk during the times Father was praying, my body became cool. During the service I recall begging God to remove the feeling I had below my knee in my left leg, which was where the first pain started, in 1961. I was asking God to remove, delay, anything or even double the pain if he so willed, but to hold off until I returned to the Bronx and home. I had the responsibility of my nephew's safety. This feeling with heat rolled from the front of my body to the back of my body all the way to my head and never stopped.

Father said we were all to get ready for the Eucharist. Then he stopped and said, "There are two people with cervical braces!"

People started to tap me on the shoulder. As I was getting up, I could hear Father saying, "Come here! I will bless you, but it's not you—just stay where you are. Come on, gang, let's go, I'm going on vacation. There are two; come, you are already healed in the name of Jesus Christ."

I started toward the door that would bring me to the stairway. When I realized my nephew might be alarmed to see me going to Father, I went back to tell him. When I got near the end of the staircase I could hardly walk with the heat in my body. Looking at the hundreds of people standing before me, it almost became an impossible dream to go forward. A lady usher then took my hand and asked me if I was hot. I was amazed at the question, as my body felt it was on fire!

She got me to the rear of the center aisle. I recalled that I saw no one as I passed the crowds. Only a great light at the front of the church was seen. Someone guided me around a body lying on the floor. It was a lady with a collar in her hands, but I did not understand why she was on the floor. When I got to Father, he was at the first pew. I assumed he had come down from the pulpit, as I had never seen him from my balcony seat. It was three hours into the service.

There was just one boy next to me. Father touched the boy's hands and looked at him and said, "My son, you also have cancer." The boy acknowledged the cancer in a spurt of emotion. Father made the sign of the cross on his forehead, and the boy's body went in a backward motion and landed on the floor. As I had never seen it before, I thanked God for having reminded me to place in each pocket of my nephew's shirt and pants his name and address, as the words of my brace maker echoed: "Don't fall with your braces on, your neck has no place to go because it is locked in and you could break it."

I was grateful my nephew was safe. So what if I was going to die, I was in church with a priest at my side. God is so good! I was delighted when the boy got up and Father instructed him to run and bend and asked him to remove his brace. He told Father that the brace was molded to his body and had to be removed by machinery.

Father then approached me, touched my hands and blessed my forehead, and my body went in a backward motion. I felt I was resting on a cloud. I was told Father prayed over me for a while on his knees, and when he stood up he asked everyone to clap for what Jesus was doing there that day, and three thousand clapped. I never heard a clap. Upon awakening, Father asked me if I had any pain.

I said, "No!" I was actually moving my left hand, arm and

both shoulders freely, which I had never done before without pain.

Father asked me, "Would you like to remove your brace?" I answered, "Yes!"

He instructed me to go up into the sacristy and remove the brace.

Upon entering the sacristy, I immediately unlocked the locks under my ears. I opened my jacket, releasing the front part of my brace, and quickly removed it over my head. I could move my head up and down, back and forth and—no pain! Hurriedly I rebuttoned my jacket, took my brace in my left hand and returned to the altar. As I walked, I kept moving my head every way, and no pain. I wore the biggest smile I could remember. I just kept moving my head.

Father came up to the altar. "Look at her!"

As he talked to me I left my brace down at the altar. Father asked me to move my head up and down, roll it, place my hands over my head. He also asked me if I had any pain. I answered, "No, Father!" in total joy. He then asked me to lift my legs up and down, which indicated he realized that I had a damaged lower spine. Then Father said I was so good, would I do some push-ups for him." Smiling I said, "I don't think I know how to!" He answered, "Just get down on your knees and spring your body forward. Go up and down."

I then realized I had not been on my knees for eighteen and a half years, and if I got down on my knees now it would be a miracle. As I knelt, a great joy came over me.

Father's feet were at my head. I held my head up to speak to him and ask him how many push-ups did he want me to do.

He said, "You just did five, that's fine!" As I rose, I started talking in great jubilation to Father, not realizing that he had a microphone around his neck. I had not seen him prior to his blessing me and it now seemed that no one else was present besides Father, the Lord and me. I said to Father, "Do you know I had four spine operations?" Surprised, he said, "Four spine operations!"

He mentioned that much damage had been done to my cervical spine. Father asked me to explain how it felt to be "slain in the Spirit." I answered that I felt it was like resting on a cloud. He then asked me to explain how it feels to be healed.

The crowd became very loud. For the first time I realized they could hear what I was saying! Father tried unsuccessfully to quiet them. I repeated that I had no pain at which point Father said, "Go praise God all the days of your life."

I left my braces at the altar and returned to the balcony. My neighbors were at the top step, waiting; and I joined them with tears of joy in my eyes.

"Gee, Aunt Nancy, you really do great at push-ups!" my nephew exclaimed in joy.

Father started to get ready for Mass, but my nephew insisted he had to have ice cream. For the sake of peace I went outside with him for a few minutes, and when he promised he would stay with my neighbor, I returned inside. I wished to attend Mass and to thank God. The greatest joy and perhaps the first realization of my healing flooded my heart when I went to receive the Eucharist, which was being distributed by Brother Laurence. I was able to open my mouth without having to place both hands down into the steel at my chin to free my chin in order that my tongue could receive the Eucharist. It was the sign I will never forget, for I was healed in Jesus' name. My braces were still lying at the altar.

Overwhelmed by God's love, we all returned to the bus and rejoiced greatly. We also heard two other healings had taken place. Midway home, my nephew asked me why I was healed and he was not. I wished somehow I could go back and pick up my braces, but I knew I could not transfer the healing to my nephew. Jesus wanted me now.

It baffled me that I went to Father DiOrio for my nephew, yet *I* was healed! Was I healed so my nephew could witness my healing? And not in Lourdes, for I was unable to take him? It was at the Feast of Pentecost Mass, seven months later, that I recollected I had asked Our Lady for a sign if she wanted me ever to return to Lourdes again. The mystery of how much God loves each of us unravels daily: how God allowed my life in braces to be noticed and touched by so many people, thus allowing his love to open so many hearts and to return souls to Himself through the loving, visible God who heals.

I know the Lord answers prayers and that it was nothing I did to deserve such a gift from God. I thank and praise God for answering my mother's intercessory prayers on earth, my father's intercession in Heaven, and for giving me such a great mother and supportive family. Our loving God not only healed me physically but also healed my memory of the pain I had suffered. It was as though God erased every trace of sickness from my mind, heart, soul and body, leaving only a great hunger for His understanding, love and compassion. The great, deeper joy and grace of knowing his loving, caring Mother, Mary, was also his gift.

A bishop once stated that when we give testimony of what the Lord has done in our lives we become a living new page in the New Testament and the Lord will bring us to places where the organized church does not and cannot go. Therefore, when Father DiOrio said to me, "Go praise God all the days of your life!" the Lord must have allotted daily situations, places, areas and people in which God's love in my life could be shared with thousands all over the United States and overseas. Never a day passes without sharing with someone what the Lord has done in my life.

The following is a letter from Dr. N————, the physician who treated Nancy Corr:

December 28, 1979

In 1961, an operation was done by me for disc removal and spine fusion using right iliac bone grafts for a herniated disc at L-5 S-1 causing left sciatic pain coming on Christmas Eve. Recovery was good.

In December of 1968 another operation was done for disc removal and spine fusion L-4 L-5 using left iliac bone grafts for herniated lumbar disc at L-4 L-5 caused by a fall in March of 1968.

In March of 1970 an operation was done for disc exploration, freeing of scarred nerve root and cervical spine fusion C-5, C-6, C-7 for disc injury caused by a fall in March of 1968. Bone bank grafts were used.

In March of 1971 an operation was done for exploration of nerve roots freeing C-6 root from adhesions and repair of failed spine fusion C-5, C-6, C-7 using right iliac bone grafts. In 1974 the fusion appeared solid C-5, C-6, C-7.

Following the operations, regular follow-up examinations were carried on until the last examination of 11/30/78 prior to my retirement from Orthopedic Surgery. At that time there remained pain in the cervical spine and left arm, numbness in the left hand with fifth finger. Some gradual improvement had occurred but there was moderately severe limitation of spinal (neck) motion and considerable disability. It was necessary to use the cervical brace that she has used for over ten years most of the time. Previously she had worn a collar for a year and a half.

When examined on 12/1/79 she was free of all neck and arm pain and numbness. Her neck and arm motions were completely normal and painless. There was no sensory or motor loss of the hand.

It was learned that this relief came immediately following a healing service by the Rev. Ralph DiOrio on September 27, 1979.

Yours truly,

Dr. N———

PRAYER:
Now, dearest Lord, as time has passed, taking away my serious bodily brokenness, I am able to realize that You do will to heal us poor mortals. I realize that sickness is not Your will, that Your children are not meant to suffer. All that You seek is that we, I, come to you with humility and in faith. You are so constantly calling, inviting each of us, just as Jeremiah 33:3 keeps reminding us, "Call to me and I will answer you." And so, dearest Lord, I called on you, and You did hear me. And as I did, I was healed of all my physical incapacities, because You, Jesus, suffered all of my illnesses. I really believe this. And in this is the power of my healing from You. Dear, dear Lord, with all my being I thank You for announcing to the world that You are the Lord, You are the healer. I am so grateful to know that Your plan for my redemption does include physical healing. With Augustine, I cry out,

"Why did You love me so much? Now I do understand what You did for me in Your great love. I thank you, Lord, for sending me, for offering to the whole world, this message of Good News.

Christine Crockett

———

MY GIFT FROM GOD

". . . Know this too: your kinswoman Elizabeth has, in her old age, herself conceived a son, and she whom people called barren is now in her sixth month, for nothing is impossible to God."

Luke 1:36

The following story indicates how nothing is impossible to God. Mrs. Christine Crockett, of Connecticut, after having spent a period of her matrimonial life as a career woman, learned at a certain point of her married life that she was now incapable of conceiving a child. This was due to scarred Fallopian tubes. Medical treatment was applied in the form of corrective surgery, but in spite of it, no assurance could be given. At that moment, a mother's cry pierced the heavens for God's gift of life. Christine prayed with all her heart to her heavenly Father. God heard that mother's prayer.

My son, Michael, was four years old already and would be going off to school in another year. I felt as though I had missed the best years of his growing up. I had been busy with my career and really enjoyed working, but now he was four and would be my baby for only one more year before school would seem to change him into a grown and independent little man.

Now I felt that I was ready to have another child. But this time I wanted to stay home and not miss any of the wonderful things that babies go through as they quickly develop from one stage to another. Since I had easily conceived the first time, I assumed that it would be just a few short months and I would be pregnant. Two months later I had an appointment with my doctor for a regular yearly exam. I was not concerned that I was not pregnant yet, because I felt that it would happen eventually. He told me that everything seemed fine and I should have no problem. So I patiently waited and didn't worry about anything.

Months went by and, before I knew it, I was back at the doctor's office for my next yearly exam. Everything seemed fine once again. Another year passed and still no pregnancy occurred. By this time, each month was a disappointment and I was beginning to wonder if I might have some type of problem. I had very long monthly cycles and sometimes pain, but assumed it was normal and just part of being a woman. When I saw my doctor, he began to ask questions and seemed more concerned. Two years had passed and the possibility of a problem had to be looked into. He took an endometrial biopsy and the results showed a discrepancy in my monthly cycle. Then he ordered a hysterosalpingogram, which is a set of X rays of the uterus, Fallopian tubes and ovaries.

I waited for about one week and then received a letter from my doctor. When I opened it, my husband was at work and Michael was in school. I just couldn't believe what I was reading! The X rays showed that both of my Fallopian tubes were blocked and I would not be able to have the baby that I was so ready for. I felt so hurt and let down, and was sure that no one would understand my feelings.

My husband did not seem upset when I told him. He felt that one child was enough and everything would be all right. I did feel blessed to have Michael. He is a beautiful child. But, for some reason, I needed more and was not ready to accept the fact that I might never conceive again.

My doctor then performed a laparoscopy. This shows exactly how much damage has been done and sometimes can even correct the problem. I was in and out of the hospital the same day and only had a few stitches, so felt it was worth my while.

Soon afterward the doctor called to ask me to come to his office for a talk. He told me that my Fallopian tubes were damaged and badly filled with scar tissue and that he could not be sure of what might have caused this. My chances of having children were one in a million. He also told me of an operation that I could have that would possibly help.

So into the hospital I went to try again. By this time I was determined! I had watched as family and friends became pregnant and gave birth, and wondered how this could have happened to me. I thought that maybe I was being punished for not spending all of my time with my son when he was a baby. I felt that I had been selfish to put my career before my own child. At this time I didn't know that God had very special plans for me. I had a lot to learn.

The night before my operation, the girl that was sharing the room with me asked if I would like to pray with her. Although I had drifted away from God, I gladly accepted, as I felt in need of Him. We prayed and talked together for quite some time and I really felt better. I knew that Jesus would take care of me.

The next morning, I had three hours of surgery and came out of it very well. The doctor was able to remove the scar tissue, but my Fallopian tubes still had some damage. He could not assure me that I would ever conceive.

During my stay at the hospital, my roommate and I searched through the Bible for help, as she also was unable to conceive. I kept praying for something to fill the emptiness that I felt by not being able to have a child. Then, during my recovery at home, I opened the Bible one day and read the first thing that hit my eyes. It was Luke 1:36–37:

Elizabeth . . . whom people called barren is now in her sixth month, for nothing is impossible to God.

I just knew that this was a message from God, and it comforted me for the time.

Months went by again, and I had done all that I could do. Now it was up to God. I felt that if He wanted me to have a child that someday I would have one. I was not going to upset myself with this any longer. Finally I had accepted the fact that I might never have another child and thanked God every day for the beautiful child that He had given to me.

Four years had now gone by when my husband came home

from work one day. He caught my interest as he told me that he worked with an usher from Father DiOrio's ministry. I had heard of Father DiOrio but did not know how to see him. My husband laughed as he told me about it, as if it were some type of circus show. I was very upset with him and said that I truly believed in God and in what Father DiOrio was doing. He could not understand how I could believe in someone that I could not see, and I knew then that he needed my prayers very badly.

I decided to send for tickets to Father DiOrio's healing service, hoping that my husband would go with me. Perhaps he would find God as I had found Him and maybe I would be healed. But when the tickets arrived he did not want to go. However, he finally agreed just to make me happy.

A month before the service, my mother and sister were injured in a car accident. As a result, my sister was left with a damaged larynx. Then I had so many things on my mind and so many people to pray for that I could no longer be concerned with my own problems.

At the healing service, I wrote one petition for my husband to receive faith and another for my sister, who was still hospitalized. The service was both beautiful and powerful, and God answered my prayer. My husband was spiritually healed! He told me that he was deeply touched and felt God's presence all over.

After the service, my husband began to come to Mass with me on Sunday and look into the Bible. Our friends could not believe the change that had come over him. He was a different man, and they all wanted to see what was responsible for this change. By now my sister was also out of the hospital, and I wanted her to attend a service. I sent for thirty tickets for the November 28, 1981, healing service, as our family and friends all wanted to go.

We felt excited to share the service with all of the people whom we love. I remember praying so hard for my sister that I felt in complete contact with God. About two hours after the service began, I experienced pins and needles in my lower abdomen. I also felt very warm. Then Father DiOrio received a "word of knowledge" that a woman dressed in orchid clothing was being healed of a problem in her Fallopian tubes. I looked around to see the person stand up and then realized that it was myself. I was wearing an orchid sweater and was so hot! The girl next to me said that I was radiating heat to her. At that moment my mother looked at me and said, "Chris, it's you." An usher walked to me and I stood up. Then Father DiOrio looked right at me and said, "That's the young lady. Come up here." I walked up to the stage and Father told me that I was being completely healed. He prayed with me and I was slain in the Spirit. When I woke up, I knew that Jesus had healed me, but I never dreamed that, one month later to the day, I would find out that I was pregnant.

My husband and I jumped for joy when the nurse said, "It's positive!" Then we cried. We were so happy! We called everyone that we knew to tell them the good news. Many of my friends had been doubters because my healing could not be seen. They had said, "When you get pregnant, then we'll believe." Well, now I was calling to tell them of my miracle.

My doctor was so thrilled and amazed at my story that he just hugged me. He believed in what had happened to me and went running out of the room to tell the nurses and other doctors.

My pregnancy came along fine, and my husband's faith grew stronger and stronger. In May 1982 he received his first Holy Communion, together with my son. This was truly a healing of the whole family.

My husband and I took natural-childbirth classes together and told everyone of our miracle. Then, on my due date, September 1, 1982, I gave birth to a beautiful and healthy seven-pound three-ounce baby girl. Certainly it had come about with the help of my husband, the doctor and God. What a miracle, we thought, as the doctor placed her in my arms right after birth. My husband had taped a picture of the broken body of Christ to the wall right in front of me. This was to be used as my focal point during labor. Each time that I looked at this picture I knew that everything would be all right. It was, and we named her Chantel Rose.

Chantel was christened three weeks later in a beautiful christening outfit that was bought by a family that we met at healing services. A week after her christening, we went to another service and Father DiOrio gave our family a special blessing. He prayed over our baby for a few minutes, anointing her with holy oil and laying his hands on her tiny head. It seems that Father finds his way over to bless Chantel each time that we go to a service. We feel strongly that somehow he knows that God has sent her to us for a special reason.

Our little miracle baby has added much joy to our lives, and God has added much faith and strength. We are grateful to Him for the love that He has shown to our family, and have become close to His Sacred Heart and Mary. Also, we are now members of the Blue Army, and my husband has recently received his Confirmation. He chose the name Thomas, because he was the doubter, as my husband was a few years ago. Jesus has really blessed our family and helped us to form a bond together in His love.

Now I know that Jesus did not want me to take for granted what it meant to be a mother. If I had conceived right away, it might not have meant as much to me as it does now. By working so hard for a second child, I came to realize the gift that I already had in my first child, as is every child that is born. Being a mother is still the second-most-important thing in my life. But now my career is no longer the first. As for me, I will serve the Lord!

PRAYER:

My dearest Lord Jesus, what a wonderful God of promises You are. You are a God of fulfillment, and nothing is impossible with You. As I look upon my little child, I cannot help but think of all the delight You take in little babes. I thank You for Your marvelous mercy. You have granted me and my husband the gift of a healthy child—when a child appeared no more to be for me. Both my husband and I can't stop thanking You, praising You for Your loving-kindness. I thank You also for the wonderful physician You sent to us. He gave us care and strength during my pregnancy and delivery. He medically sustained me to this happy moment.

Lord, I give you all the days of my life as an act of grati-

tude. Just enable me to be the kind of mother who will please You. Keep me conscious at all times of the holy trust placed in me by the gift of this child, and help me to bring this child up in the paths of Your truth and Your spirit. Send the guardian angel to watch over my little one. May that angel shelter my child from all danger of body and soul. And Lord, bless those persons who will in the future represent me as they teach and guide this wonderful gift of life that You have deigned to bless me with. O Lord, I will praise You, for I am fearfully and wonderfully made.

Kirsten Denofio

FATHER, BLESS OUR CHILD

I love those who love me;
   those who seek me eagerly shall find me.
With me are riches and honor,
   lasting wealth and justice.

                                    Proverbs 8:17–18

This is a story of two parents who would not take no for an answer from God. Continually they asked Almighty God for the grace of healing for their little, three-year-old daughter, Kirsten. Their child was suffering from "acute leukemia," which is most unpredictable in its outcome. In this tragic moment the parents persistently turned to the Lord with unfaltering prayer. They were led to a service of healing I was conducting in Albany, New York. During that service, both parents were deeply impressed by God's outpouring of grace upon His people. Encouraged at the positive blessing being witnessed, both parents were determined to receive nothing from God but his YES to their child's need. In so being determined, after the service, both parents, holding their child in their arms, personally approached me for an immediate blessing. At that moment, God took their burden; and that story is as follows.

When I think back to the first time that we went to see Father DiOrio I remember how skeptical we were. We didn't know if we were doing the right thing, but there was nowhere else to turn.

Kirsten was three and a half years old that October of 1979. She had been diagnosed as having acute lymphoblastic leukemia in January of that same year. My husband and I had planned to take her to Father DiOrio's healing service. How-

ever, the morning that we were to go she became ill. She had
been vomiting all morning and it looked as though our attendance would have to be postponed. But, to our surprise,
within a few hours Kirsten was feeling much better and
wanted to go. So in a short while we were off, and on our
way to a new beginning.

We sat and waited hopefully. Then Father DiOrio appeared. Amazed at what we saw, we soon became believers!
During the service, Kirsten became very warm and asked me
to remove her coat. After that she fell into a deep sleep. I
didn't think too much about it. As the service went on, Father
told us from the altar that many of the healings had already
begun. He said that in the next few days, when we would see
our doctors, there would be a change in our condition. We
clearly heard him say, "Leukemias will be healed."

After the service we waited to see Father. He finally came
to pray over Kirsten and simply asked, "What is wrong with
her?" As he prayed over her I looked into my husband's eyes
and they were filled with tears. I could see how much it hurt
him and how badly he wanted to see his child healed. As I
was holding Kirsten a strange feeling came over me. This
thirty-pound child that I had been holding all day became so
light, as if she had been lifted out of my hands for just a few
minutes. Then it was over and Father was gone. Afterward
Kirsten told us how hot she had felt. It was hard not to believe her, since she was only three years old.

Two days later we had an appointment with the doctor.
When he read her charts he found a favorable change in her
white blood count. Chills ran up my arms as he told me.

It was four years ago that the doctor spoke to us about
Kirsten. She has not been ill since then. That was an infinite
number of prayers ago and a lifetime of faith. It was truly a
blessing for us to have had God enter into our lives. We wish
that it hadn't been under these circumstances, but maybe
that's what it took for Him to get our attention so we could do
His work.

PRAYER:

As I come before You, dear Lord, there wells forth from my maternal heart a profound gratitude for all that You have done for my little child's healing. You have respected the persistency of both my husband's prayer and my own pleading. Psalm 62 echoes before me with those impressive words: "God alone . . . is the source of my hope." Lord, our little Kirsten had serious leukemia. And You know what that meant. Things seemed completely hopeless. Both my husband and I have left all to You, and we live in Your divine providence. Lord, we not only found peace in turning to You with persistent prayer, but we found You to remove the darkness in our lives as You healed our little Kirsten. O Lord, we cried to You in our trouble and You heard us. We praise and thank You.

Nancy Ernst

———————

PRESCRIPTION FOR HOPE

Watch Thou, dear Lord, with those who wake, or watch, or weep tonight, and give thine angels charge over those who sleep. Tend Thy sick ones, O Lord Christ: Rest Thy weary ones: Bless Thy dying ones: Shield Thy joyous ones: And all for Thy love's sake.

St. Augustine

The following story is a very impressive one. It unfolds the strength of a lovely family, closely knit in the bonds of affection, devotion and concern. Truly, a very rare vision of admiration in these days of family unrest and depersonalization. Each member of this family not only suffered together the terminal illness of cancer affecting their "heart of the home," Mrs. Nancy Ernst, but, rallying all their resources of soul and spirit, they succeeded victoriously well in utilizing not only the medical profession, but more so, with ardent unflinching faith, the Divine Healer.

Mrs. Nancy Ernst is the wife of Robert Ernst, D.M.D., of Connecticut. After the healing experience of Mrs. Ernst, both Robert and his darling wife, Nancy, dedicated their home and their own lives to the service of the sick and the suffering in a far greater dedication than ever before. Both are now also active ministry workers in our heavily attended healing sessions held in the Worcester Memorial Auditorium. May their story speak to you in its own, personal way.

October 21, 1981, was probably one of the worst days of my life. Nancy had called me with the startling news that the doctors had found a cancer that was about the size of an egg in a routine chest X ray. Four years earlier, she had been found to have breast cancer, resulting in the removal of a breast. We had lived with the fear of recurrence, but until now there had been no further signs of it. The most dangerous news was that cancer was also detected in her liver. This was the killer, because once it is in the liver the spread is rapid and death is nearby. I was stunned beyond belief! Being in the medical field, I knew the ramifications. After the phone call, I canceled patients' appointments that day and went home. Nancy and I looked at each other, communicating in the silence of our hearts. We both wanted to cry, but did not. We were showing each other how strong we were, but the tears in our hearts would not stop flowing.

In our earlier years Nancy had worked as a teacher to put me through dental and orthodontic school. I was in the Air Force for almost three years, and during that time it was a struggle just to get through in one piece. We were a childless couple and this was devastating to us. Nancy had endometriosis and underwent surgery many times to become pregnant. After twelve years of waiting for a child, we were able to adopt an infant daughter. Then, four years later, we adopted a son. We had worked hard together for so many years and were finally enjoying the fruits of our labor. I had built up an eleven-year practice as a successful orthodontist. But the most beautiful gifts that God had given to us were our eight-year-old daughter and four-year-old son. And then this deadly news was told to us.

The next morning, some more tests were to be done. I never slept that night and neither did Nancy. In the morning I slipped into another room and wept openly. I could not show my emotions to my wife or my children, because I had to be the strong one for them to lean on. Not knowing if I had enough strength to handle the situation alone, I asked our former parish priest to meet me at the hospital. Nancy and I were sitting in the hospital when Father Motta came in, and five or ten minutes later Nancy's test began. Father and I made small talk for a while. Then we silently prayed, all of the time trying to believe that this was not happening.

Then the thought of Father DiOrio popped into my mind! Thinking that we should go to see him, I turned to Father Motta and inquired if he had heard of this healing priest. He looked at me in amazement and acknowledged that the same thoughts were passing through his mind. Although he knew little about Father DiOrio, he did know people who had been to see him. He felt, along with me, that Nancy should go.

The results of Nancy's tests were far worse than we expected. The cancer was confirmed along with the need for a liver biopsy as soon as possible. Nancy was hospitalized and biopsied the following week. I'll never forget that day. Surgery was required. Several hours afterward, the doctor explained in her room that the cancer of her liver had not spread too extensively. He told Nancy that she would probably make it to 1984 and maybe even to 1986, but not to 1988. A look of despair came across her face. The only goal in her life was to raise our beautiful children, see them off and then start with our grandchildren. I saw the hurt in her eyes, but there was no anger. One must understand that to know Nancy is to love her. Not because she is my wife am I saying this. People who do come in contact with her, love her. She has a gift that draws love out of other people. But her only joy in life, the love of her children, was to be taken away from her. She was told that she would soon die and that meant that her children would be gone from her. I knew what she was thinking and then watched the tears roll down her cheeks. "God can't take me now," she said. "I have just begun to raise my children and they need me." I stood there with my heart aching.

Nancy started her hormone therapy and we searched for the best doctors and clinics. But they concurred with the original physicians and their diagnosis. So we were back to square one.

We sent for tickets for a healing service in Worcester, explaining our situation and enclosing pictures of our children. Father Motta also wrote a cover letter stating our predicament. But the service was only three weeks away and we received a letter back saying that no tickets were available. All during this time, Nancy and I prayed. I prayed myself to sleep, and at the most I would get only one to two hours of sleep a night. The other hours were spent in prayer. In fact, even between patients at the office I would sneak away and pray. Prayer was continuous. I felt my spirit talking to God, and in some way I felt Him telling me that something would happen. But being the impatient person that I am, I said, "Lord, I need something now and this can't wait." Exactly two days later, two tickets came in the mail and we were ecstatic!

On November 29, 1981, we attended a healing service with family and friends. I had never been to anything like this before. For the first time, I saw people who were slain in the Spirit falling on the floor. I didn't know what to make of it all. But I was deeply touched. During the service, the people grasped hands and raised them over their heads. I happened to be in much pain, as I had bursitis in my shoulder and couldn't raise my arms. I had to fight the people alongside of me so as not to allow them to force my arms up, as the pain was intense. I tried not to pay much attention to my pain and brushed it aside. Then Father pointed in my direction and said that bursitis was being healed and that those who were receiving a healing would feel a burning sensation in their shoulders. I heard what he was saying, but I was praying that Nancy would be called. Feeling a tingling sensation and burning, I realized what was going on. "Lord," I said, "just a minute. You have the wrong person. I didn't come for me, I came for Nancy. I can live with my pain and ailment, but she can't." At that point we began singing and raising our arms in the air. My arms went straight up, with no pain. I was healed.

Then I had a talk with Jesus. I said, "Lord, I'm not going to accept this healing, because I don't need it. Nancy needs it." Do you know the nerve Jesus had? He let me keep my healing and to this day I am trouble free.

I was bound and determined to have Father DiOrio pray over Nancy, and he walked past us several times. I got the feeling that he was avoiding us, and it made me even more determined to have him pray over her. Finally I got close enough to Father and literally shoved Nancy in front of him. He inquired about her problem and then prayed over her. She was slain in the Spirit and I leaped for joy, because I thought that she was healed. As I had been healed a half hour earlier, I knew what she was supposed to feel. I helped her up and asked her what she felt. She said that she felt nothing. I was dejected in my heart, because I knew that she was not healed. But my mother-in-law's knee was healed that day. So there was hope all around us.

In December, Nancy had pain in her neck, so we went to the hospital for further tests. The cancer had spread to her fourth vertebra, so radiation therapy was started immediately on her neck. A month later we found out that the hormone therapy was not working. So chemotherapy was started on January 5. And Nancy was failing quickly. The radiation therapy made her very sick, so that she couldn't eat or drink. The implication was that if she lived one more year she would be lucky.

Things were becoming very difficult for me. Even with the help of my mother-in-law, child rearing was becoming an increasing responsibility. I was doing more and more household chores as well as trying to keep my office together. Then a key staff member had problems of her own and left her position. I discovered that her responsibilities had not been handled properly and everything was in a shambles. The bills were rolling in, and for the first time in my life I did not have the money to pay them. I could not understand what was going on at the time, but I prayed. This is what gave me the strength to carry on.

We were scheduled to go to the next services on January 23 and 24 of 1982. During the week, a big snowstorm was forecasted. When the day arrived, the snow was coming down hard. I told Nancy, with doubt, "Gee, I don't think we'd better go. Look out the window and see all of that snow." She got my coat and boots immediately and said, "We are going!" She spoke with such determination that I didn't dare say no. I knew that she was fighting and wasn't about to give up even after what her doctors had said.

We got there with the grace of God, and we would not have made it if it weren't for our jeep. We were the first guests to enter the Marriott Hotel in Worcester, as they had just opened their doors to the public. We walked from there to the auditorium and I had to support Nancy, as she was very weak.

Fewer people came to the service because of the storm that

day, so Father DiOrio prayed over people individually. Nancy was prayed over and again felt no unusual sensation of heat. I was disappointed and once more asked the Lord to heal her. Then I made my way to the stage and lined up with everybody. Seeing Father come along, I stuck out my hands with palms down. I felt Father's hands slide under my hands, and suddenly it was as if I had taken two fingers and stuck them in an electrical outlet. I felt the electricity zap from his body into mine. Then I lost all control of my external senses and felt myself falling. A complete calmness came over me and I knew that everything was going to be all right. I lay there for a few minutes and then needed help to get up. Something wonderful had happened to me.

As we were walking back to our hotel through the snow, it crossed my mind that Father had called healings of many people who wore neck collars. Just then, Nancy looked at me and said, "Tomorrow I'll wear my neck collar." Because it caused discomfort to her jaw, she had not worn it that day. Then, at dinner, she said, "Tomorrow is my day. I'm going to be healed." Remembering my experience of knowing that everything would be all right, I looked at her and said, "Yes, tomorrow is your day."

The next day, from behind a closed curtain, Father called for a lady wearing a cranberry shirt and a neck collar. "Another neck collar," I said to myself. I knew that Nancy had a neck collar on, but all that I could see was her gray sweater. Father kept on pleading for the lady to come up and claim her healing. She didn't, so he went on calling others to come up. As he called the lady with the neck collar and cranberry shirt again, I felt an elbow tapping at my rib cage. Nancy rolled up her sweater sleeve and there was a cranberry shirt! An usher brought her to the stage, and Father prayed for a long time over her. I watched closely as tears streamed down my face.

A week later, Nancy went back to the doctor for an X ray of her neck. She was told that her neck was healing according to schedule. But the important tests would not be done until March 22. The time finally arrived, and it was a trying day. Then the call came. It was Nancy on the phone, saying in a loud and cheerful voice that the cancer in her liver was dramatically improved beyond the point when they first found it and the cancer in her chest virtually was gone. The tumor in her neck was stopped, healing on schedule. She added that when the doctors were looking at the results, they came running out saying, "Where is it?" Doctors from other floors who knew Nancy came down to look at the results in disbelief.

The repeating of tests has come and gone. The doctors have told us that Nancy is in complete remission and they are truly happy. They believe that whatever works is what really counts. Maybe there is doubt in their minds, but it doesn't bother me. I know one thing for sure about Nancy. She has been completely healed!

SUMMARY OF RADIOGRAPHIC FINDINGS:

Initial view of the cervical spine is dated 12-2-81. There is a lytic destructive process involving the body of C4. The body is widened anterior to posterior with considerable loss in vertebral height seen. Followup study dated January 1982 demonstrates partial healing with sclerosis beginning in the body anteriorly. Final film obtained July 12, 1982 reveals complete sclerosis of the vertebral body. The lytic process has filled in completely. There is no evidence of further disease within the body.

Initial lateral view of the chest is dated November 1980. No abnormality is noted. Subsequent film dated October 21, 1981 reveals an ovoid soft tissue mass anterior to the heart and just beneath the sternum. This most likely represents mediastinal adenopathy. Lesion measures 4×2 cm. Final film dated March 22, 1982 reveals disappearance of the previously described mediastinal mass. There is no evidence of residual tumor.

Howard Shapiro, M.D./jaw

PRAYER:
Lord Jesus, You are the Divine Physician; You are the Healer

of mankind. In some fashion, I, too, know what pain is; and with Your grace, I have attempted to ease the pain of another by my own respective medical profession. As two physicians, Lord, we both understand "treatment" and "cure." We both rejoice when health is given to the body, to the spirit, and to the soul's psychic and emotional needs. Nobody on earth can ever "buy" health of body, wholesomeness to the mind, and peace to the soul. But, Lord, I especially appreciate Your particular grace to me, who have become all the more impressed with the anguish of pain and the possibility of death. What a traumatic shock that is—especially when such a destructive illness threatens the one you love. My dear darling wife, Nancy, was at that point. We did all we could, all that was medically and reasonably possible. But most of all, we prayed to You. *Thank You, Lord. You not only heard our cry, but You blessed our family with more love and devotion, more unity and loyalty. Nancy was healed. She is Your* continued gift *to our lives. Yes, dear Lord, You are our "PRESCRIPTION OF HOPE."*

Florence Fillion

THE TENDER HEALER

Yes, as the clay is in the potter's hand, so you are in mine . . .

Jeremiah 18:6

It is always interesting how God speaks to His souls. So very often what appears to be a tragedy of anguish turns out in the long run to be one of God's invitations of grace. As one reads the story of Florence Fillion, one cannot help but see how the Almighty God used human pain as a "stepping-stone" of grace for personal interior renewal. Everybody loves "new beginnings." And in Florence's case, in 1979, God gave her just that. God used pain to touch her soul. So many of us never seem to realize that the "best is yet to be," especially and even more so when we are placed in the hands of the Almighty Potter.

For many years I had a hard lump on the back of my heel. It was large and my foot would get swollen. But I never gave too much thought to it until the summer of 1975, when it became difficult to walk and maintain my balance.

Our family doctor thought that it could be bursitis. Although he felt that medical treatment might help, he referred me to an orthopedic surgeon. I saw the X ray showing a chipped bone under my heel. The doctor gave me cortisone treatment and asked me to consider having surgery. It was to be a simple operation, with only a few days in the hospital, and a walking cast would be applied to my ankle. Little did I know that it would be a long time before I would again wear high-heeled shoes.

But what was to be a half-hour operation turned into almost three hours. I was conscious most of the time and there seemed to be a lot of confusion. Then I fell asleep. When I awoke there was a heavy cast from my toenails to my hip. The doctor said that chipped bone was mixed in the nerves and muscles. He was sorry, but a benign tumor had necessitated the cutting of a main tendon. He spoke with my husband and apologized for what he felt he had to do. He told him that I wouldn't be crippled, but . . . and left it like that.

I spent three weeks in the hospital. First I used a wheelchair and then a walker. Eventually arrangements were made for me to go home by ambulance. I couldn't climb stairs, so a hospital bed was set up in our den. It was a year and a half of slow progress before I finally graduated to a cane. Over all of this time I became very bitter. Although the tumor was gone I was worse off after the operation than I had been before.

My husband is a police officer in our town, and one day someone told him of chartered buses to Father DiOrio's services. We made plans to be passengers on the next bus that was bound for Worcester. It was April of 1979, and I went to the service reluctantly, never thinking of a healing for myself. I was praying for my sister, who was ill with arthritis. During that service, as Father was blessing the people, he put his hand on my head and prayed, "Lord, bless this woman with a leg injury."

I did a lot of thinking when I got home, and knew that I had to go back. In a few weeks we returned again to find the church overcrowded. Out of necessity I climbed stairs to the balcony. As we began to pray my body burned. Suddenly I felt an urge to get up and walk. Without giving my cane a thought, I rose from my seat and began to walk. I walked back and forth, and up and down. I knelt. I stood. I ran. I praised God, for I was healed!

It was a different person who returned home. I began to clean and paint and use a stepladder. Everyone wondered what had happened to me when I went to Mass in our parish. I no longer struggled up the stairs to the church, using my cane and holding on for dear life to the railing. My doctor shook his head in wonder at what I could do.

Several years have passed and my heel is stronger than ever. I read Scripture daily and spend an hour in prayer. To God I will be forever grateful. He touched me and made me whole.

PRAYER:
Dear Lord, sometimes I can be very upset about the things that happen to us mortals. At times, this upsetness can even turn into nastiness. How cruel that type of attitude can be! Yet, on the other hand, Lord, when one experiences such feelings, that, too, can be used as a grace for introspection. I know "someone" . . . You know her too . . . don't You, Lord? In fact, amusingly reflecting on her, we both know that "someone" to be ME. Forgive me, Lord, for my foibles, my anger, my bitterness. Oh, the price of woe we mortals must pay! We need You, Lord, to be our Healer. You are our Truth, our Life, our Way. Are not the words of Leslie Savage Clark so true when he states that a Healer's hands were there in Galilee. "They were stretched to all who came to Him. From Him they sought the cleansing of hidden wounds." Thank You, Lord. You not only touched with Your healing hands the pain of my body, but with Your healing wounds you redeemed my mortal heart for YOU as well as FOR ME.

Pauline Fleishman

———◆———

WHEN THE PAIN IS BAD

My grace is enough for you: my power is at its best in weakness. . . . For it is when I am weak that I am strong.

2 Corinthians 12:9–10

When one knows Jesus, really and truly knows Him, one has a strength beyond all human description. In fact, one can "handle" any devastation that attempts to strike our human existence. In the case of Pauline Fleishman, the tragedies in life fell upon her as hurricanes sweep to naught the lands they engulf. Pauline experienced the pangs of separation through the loss of her three-year-old-child abruptly, causing the anguish of personal grief to eat away any inner trust and peace. Furthermore, following the latter suffering of human desolation, Pauline suddenly found that life was to be still harder on her: she found herself the victim of breast cancer, with recurring malignancy. Surgery was even contemplated. It seemed that she was hemmed in from all sides by stark walls of pain. It was almost more than she could bear. To whom was she to turn? Religion, thank God, is not life; it is only a key to Him Who is life. Somehow, God's grace brought Pauline to communicate all the more with her God. In Him she found the strength that both her body and her soul needed.

All of my life I had always felt that I was a religious person. I could boast of having been at Sunday Mass for fifteen years running. And didn't I kneel to say my prayers each night? Just consider all of the novenas that I made to our Blessed Mother. Oh, yes, I knew that there was a God. But I was

never really sure that He knew me. Ours was a very imper-
sonal relationship.

In 1963 I lost Susan. My beautiful little girl was just shy of
three. People had remarked that she looked like an angel. I
guess it was true. They called it "galloping pneumonia" and
she was taken abruptly. For seven years I mourned that child.
I could neither look at her picture nor say her name. Certainly
it was the most devastating time of my life. Had I known
Jesus, it could have been different.

Eight years after the death of my child, I found myself undergoing a radical mastectomy for cancer of the breast. It
was another very difficult time for me. I was a frightened
woman for five years, the time required to determine if I had
conquered the disease. When it was over, my husband and I
went out to celebrate. Then my doctor cautioned me against
being too optimistic. There was a 20 percent chance of recurrence within the next two years. Again, if I had only known
Jesus Christ!

It was at this time that I became aware of the charismatic
renewal within the Church. A friend took me to a home
where a group of women were meeting for prayer and Bible
study. I returned for several weeks, as I found such a peace
there. Then I was directed to a seminar where I was "bap-
tized in the Spirit." This was the beginning of a new life for
me.

Two years went by and I returned to my doctor. Not liking
the looks of scar tissue, he proceeded to take a biopsy. When
the report came back, it showed a recurrence of malignancy.
This was a few days before Thanksgiving in 1978. After our
holiday dinner, I entered the hospital to have surgery the next
day.

I was well aware that this stay differed from my previous
one. Jesus was with me, and I was soon able to recognize His
presence. The first night, I was awakened in my room as I felt
a hand under my chin. The words "chin up" came to me and I
opened my eyes, fully expecting to see a nurse in my room.
But there was no one there. The following night, the same
thing happened except that the motion and words were much
more forceful. When I opened my eyes, there was no one

there. Although I hadn't thought too much of it the first night, the second time I couldn't dismiss it lightly. Then, on the third day, as I was drifting in and out of sleep, I saw the head and shoulders of a man at the foot of my bed. He stretched out his arm the length of the bed and put his hand under my chin. Again I heard "chin up," and there was no doubt in my mind that God was with me.

Some nights later, I stopped in the corridor to speak with a woman that I vaguely recognized. Her brother had been brought in for emergency surgery and together we spoke of that. When I left her, she said, "Pauline, keep your chin up." Again, as I left the hospital a young nurse sat on my bed, and said, "Mrs. Fleishman, you keep your chin up." I had such a peace in that hospital. In my pursuit of the Lord I had met so many good people, and I was secure in their prayer.

Three weeks after surgery, I went to my doctor for what I thought was a routine checkup. It was then that I learned that "extensive growth" had been found. Scrapings had been sent to Boston, and they recommended a removal of the adrenal gland. I was upset and decided to wait, making another appointment for after Christmas.

My husband and I decided that I should see a specialist in Albany, so we scheduled a date for after New Year's. In the meantime, I saw my own doctor after having made the decision that I would not submit to surgery again. But before I could say anything to him, he informed me that he had decided to postpone my surgery for a few weeks, as he wanted to put me on a drug instead. It was then that I told him that I had no intention of having further surgery, as I was expecting a divine healing. What I did not know at this time was that he had prepared my family for my death, within a few months.

On April 5, 1979, I boarded a bus for Worcester, Massachusetts, to attend a healing service of Father Ralph DiOrio. We sat in the balcony, and at one point Father called for those with cancer. He mentioned several people on the lower level of the church and one lady in the balcony who was dressed in beige and purple. I could relate to the beige but not to the purple and I cried, thinking that I had lost my chance.

Several women on the lower level had gone up for their

healings. Later in the evening, Father asked again for the lady in the balcony with the cancer, pointing in the area where I was sitting. He repeated the color beige and again mentioned that she had purple on. It was then that it hit me. He didn't say that I was wearing purple, but rather that I had it on me.

I must go back to the morning when we left. It was very early and I had taken one of my husband's large handkerchiefs and some Kleenex. But just before my ride showed up I had decided that I had better get another hankie. I went into our bedroom and saw that my husband had gone back to bed. Not wanting to awaken him by crossing the room to his drawer, I took a handkerchief from my drawer, close to the door. I know that the Lord arranged it in this way, because if I had seen the hankie that I selected, I would never have taken it. It was solid purple!

From as far back as I can remember, the color purple has always frightened me, reminding me of death. I can't really account for this except that I have seen it in coffins so often and draped around Our Lord at Easter time. As I was hurrying out to catch my ride to the bus that day, I slid the hankie into my pocket and caught sight of the purple. I was really puzzled. "Lord," I questioned, "how could you give me a death omen to take to a healing service? So be it."

It was when Father called for the purple the second time that I remembered my purple hankie and waved it from my seat in the balcony. Father said, "That's the color I'm looking for. Is that part of your regalia?" He asked me some questions and then prayed over me. As I was overpowered by the Holy Spirit, I heard him say, "She is being healed." I knew in that moment that God was with me and that my healing was complete.

When I arrived home that evening, my husband was waiting up for me and I told him what had happened. I'm not really sure how much he believed, but I know that he was happy for me. The following morning I couldn't decide what I should be doing first, so I asked the Lord, "Should I get up on the rooftop and tell the world?" Then I said, "Lord, I'm going to Your word and, as always, speak to me at the very top of the page so there is no question in my mind that it is meant for me." My Bible opened to Isaiah 42:1 at the top of the page: "Behold my servant. . . . He shall not cry, nor lift up, nor cause his voice to be heard in the street." I responded: "Okay, Lord, I keep my mouth closed until I hear from You."

The following morning, I was still in somewhat of a daze, wondering if I had dreamed or imagined it all. I went to the Lord again and asked that He reassure me that I wasn't dreaming. I opened His word to the Third Epistle of John 1–3 "The elder unto the wellbeloved. . . . Beloved, I wish above all things that thou mayest prosper and be in health, even as thy soul prospereth. For I rejoiced greatly when the brethren came and testified of the truth that is in thee, even as thou walkest in the truth."

That evening, my husband came home from the school where he teaches and handed me a mimeographed paper to read. I was upset when I read it. It was a rundown on my healing that he had distributed throughout the school. He felt, because they had been praying for me, that they were entitled to know. I said, "Oh, David, the Lord told me not to open my mouth." "I know," he said, "but He didn't say anything to me." I understood then why I wasn't to go out into the streets. The Lord was going to do it His way.

It was Holy Thursday and I was listening to our parish priest read the Passion of our Lord. He mentioned the purple cloak that was put on Him before the crucifixion. At that moment, I had such an awakening that left no doubt in my mind about the color purple. Purple was not death. Purple was life. The Lord had used that color purple not only in healing me physically but in healing me of the dread of that color.

When I thought back on the way in which purple had been used, I realized that the Lord had been preparing me. While I was in the hospital, my sister had brought me a little gift. It was a decorative glass folder covered with deep-purple flowers. I did not like it, so put it in a spot at home where I would not see it too often. Then, when I was home recuperating, my daughter's girlfriend brought me an African violet, my least favorite plant. It had two small purple flowers on it. I hated it, so I put it in my son's room, where I did not have to look at it.

Shortly after my healing, that plant blossomed out and was covered with the most beautiful purple flowers.

The week after my healing, I was sitting in the backyard when the telephone rang. As I ran across the lawn to answer it, I stopped abruptly. There, in the middle of the lawn, was one lone purple flower. I don't know how it got there, as we had no flowers growing in our backyard. I picked it, knowing it was a love letter from the Lord, reassuring me of His love and His presence. The following week, I had a few neighbors in. One, who walked from her house, stopped by the roadside and picked two purple flowers, which she gave to me when she came in.

It has been close to four years since my healing. I have seen my doctors every three months up to the present time. Each visit has included all kinds of tests, X rays, blood work-ups. I have had body scans yearly. My X rays showed a steady improvement over the months until one of my doctors said, "There is no evidence of disease."

I thank God every day of my life for His goodness and His mercy. He has given me peace and joy. Yes, he has given to me His healing love.

PRAYER:
Dear Lord and Saviour Jesus, Your mercy and Your love are so much one. In fact, You are extended to this earth through those virtues. Your power is like the wideness of the sea, so ready to engulf, to enrapture me. I needed so desperately Your kindness. You showed me that kindness as soon as I raised my weaknesses to You. Your mercy and Your love showered themselves upon me. You gave me the comfort I needed. The tenderness of Your hands soothed me. I drank deeply of Your living waters. You quenched me with the springs of Your healing love. Healed in both body and spirit, I now rest peacefully in the labors of my earthly days, in the cool serenity of Your Divine Presence.

Nora Hickey

———

OPEN MY EYES, LORD, I WANT TO SEE

But until today Yahweh has given you no heart to understand, no eyes to see, no ears to hear.

Deuteronomy 29:4

One of the greatest tragedies of life is that which dies within us while we live. All of us experience a deep need to love; but, at the same time, the need to be loved in return is all the more profound. The heart of Christ Himself experienced the anguish of rejection from those He loved. Some believe that Jesus died of a broken heart, not so much from the lance that pierced His sacred heart upon his expiration but more so because those whom He loved had not returned love for love. If God could feel this pain, how much more can we fathom that rejection, we who on earth thrive and survive on that basic craving of which we are slaves: the need to be loved. How all-the-more painful it must be when we live for someone, with someone, but are never sure if he or she really loves us. That is a torment beyond description. Nora Hickey, a lovely Irish immigrant, living and working in New York, expresses these aspects in her narration. It is truly interesting to see how God speaks to her and renews his love to her by removing her partial blindness. Sometimes in life we cannot hear God speaking to us about His constant love unless we experience His presence. What greater impact can God make on us than when He touches the sick unto healing?

Since childhood, my favorite story has been that of the woman who touched the garment of Jesus and was healed. I, too, was blessed by such an experience. In June 1979, at St.

John's Church, in Worcester, Massachusetts, I received a healing of my eyes and a renewal of my life.

My eye problem started at the age of seven. I had a lazy left eye and perfect vision in the right eye. The doctor suggested glasses and an eye patch to be worn for one hour each day, giving strength to the weak eye. Being a wild farm kid, I never wore the eye cover and rarely wore the glasses. Excessive reading would later weaken my overworked right eye.

Part of this story is on forgiveness. Previous to 1970, I had known a very happy life both in Ireland and in America. I had known good people. I also had loved God in a very special way but doubted His special love for me.

In an apartment house on the East Side of New York City I became a lady superintendent, having complete charge of painting and maintenance. Like the painted sepulcher, the building was a type of Sodom and Gomorrah. So, for the next six years, I was to suffer the hate and maliciousness of very violent and evil people. The few that were good kept silent. I pleaded with God to protect me. He did, in the form of wonderful police and an unusual gift of a Bible that I found in a dustbin in the street. I devoured its words and learned that Jesus loved these people and that He died on a cross for their sins. So one day I would forgive them all. It took a lot of forgiveness.

In 1978, glare bothered my eyes, and once in a while a dark shadow would appear on my left eye. The muscle was weak. One day, after spending some hours at the eye doctor's and receiving no kindness, I went to a restaurant and talked to God over my coffee. Pleading with Him to heal my eyes, I promised Him that I would always do His will. The following year, my prayer was answered—through the medium of Father DiOrio.

The healing service was over. My glasses in my bag, I was loaded down with two coats as well as bags belonging to friends. Father DiOrio was returning unexpectedly from the lower church, so we couldn't get out with the crowd to our waiting New York-bound bus. From twenty feet away, Father came toward me and prayed over my eyes. It seemed as if I were struck by lightning! As though holding on ever so tightly to the hem of the garment of Jesus, I repeated over and over again, "Jesus, I love You. . . . I'm sorry. . . . Forgive me." His presence was overpowering and my heart was filled with love. The words came back so clearly: "But I do love you. . . . Believe Me! I do love you." Looking into my eyes, Father DiOrio asked me how I felt. His face was sheer compassion. He blessed my eyes again, and once again the presence of Jesus became so very real to me as I was aware of a sensation of brightness. The words of love came back, saying, "I love . . . but I do love you."

As I stood on my feet, I was different. I was transformed. My mind was renewed. I could see better. I could hear better. And I loved with a new love. I held my hands to my heart. It was all so fast and unexpected. The next morning, something like fish scales came out of my left eye. The muscle was completely healed, all glare disappeared, and my eyes have never bothered me since. In addition, 80 percent of my sight was restored through this healing, leaving me with a need to wear glasses only for small print.

To know God is to live. For me it's a joy! I love my present work, with the talented and the glamorous people of the perfume world, where I can have fresh roses each day for my desk. It's also a joy to help runaway kids at Covenant House, in Times Square, and share my food with a teenager who has never known love. Like St. Paul, I received a conversion. So much like St. Peter, Jesus molded me into a rock. I received the gifts of faith and love. He even reached down and allowed me to touch the hem of His garment.

PRAYER:
Then from behind him came a woman, who had suffered from a hemorrhage for twelve years, and she touched the fringe of his cloak, for she said to herself, "If I can only touch his cloak I shall be well again." Jesus turned around and saw her; and he said to her, "Courage, my daughter, your faith

has restored you to health." And from that moment the woman was well again.

Matthew 9: 20–22

Dear Jesus, I know that to have sight does not mean that one can see. To have a heart does not mean one can love. To have ears does not mean one can hear. I praise You, my Lord, for healing my eyes and giving me new vision, Your vision. I praise You for healing my heart and for giving me forgiveness and love. How can I express my gratitude? I will stay close to You, Sweet Healer, all the days of my life, knowing that You continue to walk with me. And one day You will lead me to my eternal home in heaven with You, where I can praise You forever and ever. Amen.

Frank J.

———

THE MAN WITH FIVE
ACCIDENTS

. . . with him alone for my rock, my safety, my fortress, I can never fall.

Psalm 62:2

"I thank God for my recovery" is a sentence not lightly said by Frank J., from Cleveland, Ohio. His story is unique. Frank experienced a very unusual form of illness. If one were to read his narration of accidents, one would just about call Frank "accident-prone." But regardless of the five traumatic accidents upon his body, today Frank is able to express deep satisfaction and gratitude for restored health. He is able to look back at the times of his accidents, four by automobile and one from five hundred pounds of stock falling upon him. Now healed completely, and enjoying life to its full, Frank looks back upon those incapacitated, injury days as a time in which he grew in trust of God and in the love God manifested to him through those who cared, and those who prayed.

It was a long history of illness that brought me to the Convention Center, in Cleveland, to see Father DiOrio. Sixteen years previously I had been injured in a car accident. At that time I had received a compressed cervical fracture. Then, the very next year, five hundred pounds of stock had fallen on top of me, resulting in a fractured lumbar vertebra. When examining me, my doctor had also discovered a birth defect in this area, and somehow I had managed to injure my neck again.

In 1979 I was in another car accident, reinjuring my neck and back. Within a period of two years I underwent three back surgeries, during which time a severed nerve to my left leg resulted in a loss of feeling in half of my foot and the calf of my leg. Then, in August of 1982, I was involved in a third car accident, further injuring my back and neck and occasioning additional surgery to my back. Unbelievable as it may sound, a month prior to going to the healing service, I was in a fourth accident, when a car in which I was riding was hit from the rear. This time I sustained a whiplash injury, bruised ribs and shoulders, and head and back injury.

In early April of 1983 I went to the Convention Center. At the time, I was in pain and unable to move freely. I wore a back and neck brace as well as a rib belt, and also walked with a cane.

After leaving the Convention Center I attended a dinner for Father DiOrio. While walking out the door of the restaurant I saw him about to get into his car. I proceeded to approach my own car, when he came up to me and inquired about my injury. He took my cane, removed my neck brace and blessed my neck. As he did, I felt a warm, tingling sensation going through my left side. Then he touched my head and I was slain in the Spirit. I could hear people talking around me, but Father DiOrio did not speak. Although I tried to open my eyes, I could not, until I came to.

It was cold outside but I was very warm and perspiring. My neck moved with no pain. My head, ribs, shoulders and back no longer hurt. For the very first time in close to two years I had feeling in my left calf and foot. I was able to walk without my cane and with no pain. I couldn't believe what was happening to me! And then again, I could.

My doctor had advised me that the whiplash injury could last anywhere from four weeks to four months. Two weeks later, when Father prayed with me, it went away. The doctor had also said that other nerves in my leg could take over the sensation of the severed nerve. But it had not happened. He also stated that my back would take one to two years to heal following surgery. But none of this had occurred and I was in pain. Then, on April 10, 1983, it all happened at once. God healed me through the prayer of Father DiOrio.

Today all of the areas of my body that had sustained injury are just fine. Nine days after I received my healing, an X ray of my back merely showed slight arthritis due to the severe strain and surgeries that I had undergone. But this area is improving every day.

Surely all of these things that my doctor said related to my recovery could have happened. But they did not. Rather, it all came about at once on April 10, 1983, at 10:30 P.M. in a parking lot in Cleveland, when Father DiOrio blessed me. Nothing will make me believe otherwise. I was in pain and now I am not. It was not a matter of time. Rather, it was my time to be touched by God!

PRAYER:
Dear God, I thank You for my recovery. As I look back upon all those ugly accidents, when I think of that five hundred pounds of stock falling upon me, I almost think it is incredible that I am here to thank You. I place before my inward eyes those drastic tragic moments. They seem so alive in my memory, in my pain experienced! My body, my soul, all my powers seemed fatally terminated. What frustrations I experienced, what fear I voiced in that time of brokenness! So many people came in their own name; some came in Your name to console me. But then, one Sunday evening, You Yourself came. You heard my feeble cry for help. Your dear servant priest came up to me. He spoke Your tender concern. He touched me with Your compassionate hand. Your Holy Spirit permeated my entire being with the warmth of Your healing love. How strange that moment felt; almost as strange as the accidents. But that moment was real! Today I thank You with all my heart. Healed anew, I will walk afresh in Your truth and in Your spirit.

Jack H. Klie, M.D.

———◆———

THE DOCTOR WHO CAME
TO THE DIVINE PHYSICIAN

My son, when you are ill, do not be depressed,
but pray to the Lord and he will heal you.

Ecclesiasticus 38:9

Honor the doctor with the honor that is his due
in return for his services;
for he too has been created by the Lord.

Ecclesiasticus 38:1

Then let the doctor take over—the Lord created him too—
and do not let him leave you, for you need him.
Sometimes success is in their hands,
since they in turn will beseech the Lord
to grant them the grace to relieve
and to heal, that life may be saved.

Ecclesiasticus 38:12–14

*The greatest intelligent man is not he who categorizes librar-
ies of knowledge within his brain, but he who is humble
enough to know that the authentic perceptive man is he who
realizes that he knows not everything. Moreover, the sign of
an intelligent man is not that he analyses data alone, but that
he knows how to synthesize that knowledge into the wisdom
of objective living.*

The following case narration describes a very learned
medical man, Jack H. Klie, M.D., cardiologist, from Providence, Rhode Island. Doctor Klie had suffered for fifteen
years with the excruciating crippling disease of rheumatoid
arthritis. The extent of the illness led to the use of crutches
and threatened him with the loss of independence. This interfered with his life's vocation, dedication to the sick. Further diagnosis indicated that he would be in need of a hip
replacement, which would cause him to be out of his practice
for six consecutive months or so. At that moment of decision,
and with the inspiration of friends, Dr. Klie gave his illness
to the Lord, the Divine Physician. Any man who remembers
God as the Author of life retains that God in his own life both
as Divine Giver of life and Divine Physician of healing.

One day, Dr. Klie and his dear wife attended a healing
service at the Worcester Memorial Auditorium, under the direction of the Apostolate of Prayer for Healing and Evangelization. During that service, Dr. Klie was awestruck at observing concretely and realistically the divine power of his

God working through a simple priest. For six hours during that service, Dr. Klie scrutinized the strange but awesome beauty of a loving Miracle-God, while observing every move that I made. People from all walks of life were there: every nationality and creed. Love and respect for human beings were definitely present. And this was not feigned. People were so moved as they realized that God was not some old traditional recorder of good marks and bad marks. Rather, they experienced God as a loving Father Who came to bless His people. And one of those blessings was in healing. People with all types of illnesses were observed as they presented themselves to the service; and all types of illnesses found their blessings of healing. God did not want His people sick, He was not the author of sickness and disease; but He wanted His people well, healthy and blessed.

This holy atmosphere began to be the tool of the Divine Physician to heal a gifted medical man, Dr. Klie. Upon leaving that auditorium that day, Dr. Klie received a deep inner awakening. God was working from within this scientifically trained cardiologist to accomplish the external healing of his body.

En route to their home in Providence, Rhode Island, Dr. and Mrs. Klie stopped off at a restaurant. God's grace is always working, no matter where the place may be. God loved Dr. Klie. God was calling Dr. Klie to higher visions and graces for both his own, personal soul and for his beloved profession as cardiologist. At that restaurant, who do you think entered along with some friends for dinner? It was myself. And there at that restaurant, the doctor and I were introduced. Seeing the man still on crutches but with a renewed inner spirit glowing all over his being, I asked the doctor if he wished to be blessed. And with that blessing, God actualized the story of "The Doctor Who Came to the Divine Physician."

I am a physician and have had arthritis for almost fifteen years. My knees used to fill up with so much fluid that they had to be tapped about every month. This usually would be followed by cortisone injections. I was unable to bend my knees without these treatments. Two years ago my hips became so painful, with such a limited range of motion, that I was forced to use crutches. I proudly resisted the idea of crutches until walking became almost impossible without them. I would step a few inches at a time. Ascending one step was a major challenge. Illness teaches humility.

The medications I was taking for my arthritis produced ulcers in my intestinal tract, and I often stayed up at night nursing severe abdominal pain. Sometimes I had no choice but to stop the arthritis medication. My doctors told me that I would need to have both hips replaced and that I would also need corrective surgery for a deformed ankle. Chemotherapy was also discussed. It would take about six months before I could go back to my medical practice after building up my leg muscles postoperatively.

The alternatives that were available to me were frightening and I certainly did not want to leave my practice, even for six months. I started to pray. People started to pray for me. Sometimes these prayers came from unexpected sources, and this touched me. Finally, my wife and my mother-in-law convinced me to see Father Ralph DiOrio. I went to one of his healing services in October of 1981.

When entering the great hall where he was to preach, I was immediately struck with awe. I felt the presence of God there. It was a deeply emotional experience, seeing the power of Christ expressed through Father Ralph's loving and healing touch for six hours. Many people were healed during that service. Father did not touch me. He remained on the other side of the room, surrounded by a crowd of people. I was not physically healed then, but this did not matter, because the spiritual awakening in me was more important.

That evening, a miraculous turn of events occurred. While traveling home, which was an hour away, we decided to stop for supper. It took about half an hour to reach the restaurant. As we ordered dinner, we joked that maybe Father DiOrio would eat in the same place and perhaps I would finally meet him after all. As we were halfway through our meal, my stepson remarked that Father DiOrio was indeed coming in the

door. Joe is a natural prankster and I laughed it off until none
other than Father DiOrio entered the room with a large en-
tourage and sat down at the table next to us. We were too
embarrassed to interrupt his meal, but Joe had the courage to
leave him a note written by my wife asking him to pray for
me. As she and I started for the door, Father DiOrio immediately summoned us over to his table and asked me about my
affliction. He then prayed over me and told me that I would
feel better after a restful sleep that night. It was then that I
received the partial healing that marked the beginning of my
progressive recovery.

The following week, I returned to work without crutches
and walked rapidly up and down the halls of the hospital,
making my rounds. Since that day my knees have never again
accumulated fluid. I no longer have ulcers and can take my
arthritis pills without getting stomach pain. I am able to continue my practice without any limitations. My patients and
colleagues were amazed at the change in my condition. The
only time that my rheumatologist sees me is when I wave to
him in the halls of the hospital or discuss a patient with him.

I am not totally cured of arthritis but believe that I may be
completely healed someday. I think that God has left some
residual disease in me so that I will get closer to Him. When I
reach that next spiritual plateau, I may be rid of this disease
completely. However, I have come to realize that these are
God's choices and not ours. He decides if and when we are to
be healed and in what manner. Those of us in the profession
of healing often have to be patient and not expect too much
at once. I am very happy and, like a good patient, plan to
return for follow-up.

PRAYER:
Lord of all health and life, I come before You with a grateful
soul and heart, that by Your grace I have been called to serve
your people as a healer of bodies. Help me and all my col-
leagues to penetrate the miraculous powers hidden in the
mysteries of Your created world. May we respect the gift of
prolonging life, never taking it away.

Lord, You are the Divine Physician, You bring holistic healing to all mankind. Humbly grateful for Your thoughtfulness to me by Your healing touch, I turn to You. I ask You to inspire me to see in every pain Your holy presence, that in serving others it really is You, O Lord, to Whom I minister. In Your abundant mercy, continue to bless me with this restored life both to my "inner spirit" and to my "external body." Take me, Lord, receive me as Your channel of healing.

M. Ann Lambert

———◆———

I REALLY THOUGHT I HAD
IT MADE

Take pity on me, God, take pity on me,
in you my soul takes shelter;
I take shelter in the shadow of your wings
until the destroying storm is over.
I call on God the Most High,
on God who has done everything for me. . . .

Psalm 57:1–2

How would you feel if your doctor had just given you the bad news, as gently as he could, that you will probably not recover from an ovarian cancer? Immediately, you become frightened with loads of trembling questions and fears. You do not know how much time you have left. Such was the experience of M. Ann Lambert. Contented at a certain point of her life, having achieved what she would consider "a sense of well-being" about the directions that her life had taken, M. Ann Lambert was suddenly shocked at the news that her life could terminate abruptly. And in the meantime, she would have to make drastic changes in her life. A malignant tumor had disrupted her health. The shock was dismaying. She felt anger at an intrusion and invasion by some unkindly force, some dark power, some thief spirit shortening her days. Through a host of tears, she wondered if she would be cured. What she really was asking was if she would live.

It was Good Friday 1981. As my heavy eyelids pushed their way open, I saw a kind, soft-spoken doctor bending over me to tell me the news. "We removed a tumor," he said. "Was it malignant?" I asked, barely managing to mouth the slurred words. "Yes," he responded, "but with today's new treatment for this type of ovarian cancer, we can extend your life by ten years, if you will submit to it." I closed my eyes and rolled my head over to make the doctors and anyone else that was present believe that I had fallen back into my drug-induced sleep.

My mind raced with all sorts of thoughts. Why did it have to be a tumor? The doctor had said that it could be adhesions that had caused the pain, or just the disease of the ovary itself, worn out like all of the other organs that had been removed many years before. Seven children (no, eight, counting the little angel that had been miscarried early in pregnancy several years ago) take quite a toll on a woman's body. And if it had to be a tumor, why did it have to be malignant? Didn't my general doctor tell me that 70 percent of the tumors that are found in surgery are not malignant?

Ten years! Big deal! I had reached the point in my life where I thought that I had really made it. I had a good family and I loved my latest job, which had given me just the measure of prestige that I had always wanted. With Jim's income, we were finally at a point where we could look forward to a wonderful retirement that we were already planning. Ten years. . . . I would not even live to see that retirement. In fact, ten years was only promised in cases in which this "new" treatment worked. Otherwise, according to the doctors, I had six months to live.

"O God," I prayed, "I know that my family really needs me. My baby is only fifteen. But, God, I can't go through what they put my sister through. I cannot burden my family with this trial either. Tell me what I should do."

On the last day of my hospital stay I finally agreed to undergo chemotherapy. I was scheduled for fourteen treatments, to be given twenty-one days apart. As I lay there undergoing treatment throughout those many hours, I could not speak to anyone, as it brought on vomiting. I didn't want to talk anyway. I just wanted to be left alone. There was nothing to do but to pray. And I spent my time doing just that. Watching the clock, I would count off the hours when I knew that the vomiting might stop. Then I would measure off the twenty-four-hour period that it took to feel up to walking around without assistance. I did this knowing that soon I would be back in my own home, away from a place that seemed to be more and more like a prison where torture took place.

After eight such treatments I developed a condition called polyneuropathy, or dead nerves in my hands and feet. No longer able to endure what it was doing to me either physically or mentally, I quit treatment. I had reached the point where I would become sick to my stomach for a week preceding treatment. It was difficult for me to eat and I was losing a great deal of weight. Sitting was painful, since I had little flesh to cover my bones, which ached upon contact with even the most softly cushioned chairs. Lying down was even more painful, as more bones came into contact with the surface than when sitting. Walking was hard too, and driving became impossible.

For several months I had been driving while this condition existed. But as the illness progressed, one day I found that my foot could not find the brake and I nearly crashed through a brick wall. When I reported this to the doctor who was treating the polyneuropathy, he said that he was not aware that I was still driving or he would have advised against it. Nevertheless, between the mental anguish and the thought of becoming a cripple for my family to be saddled with, I had lost my will to live. My mind was in a desperate state and I was supposed to report to the doctor on that day of December 18, 1981, for my ninth chemotherapy treatment. First I called the doctor and told him that I would not be there for treatment on either that day or any other. Then I called a priest from the nearby church that I had begun to attend because I was no longer able to walk to my own parish, a block away. Truthfully, I was just barely able to make it to this church with my cane.

The priest assured me that I was not committing suicide by quitting, and this had been my greatest fear. I could not despair and commit such a terrible sin against the God Whom I still trusted and loved so much. After all, He is the God Whom I sincerely felt that I would be meeting much sooner than I had planned before all of this happened to me. The priest, however, tried to persuade me to reconsider and go back to treatment. He told me of a secretary in a rectory where he had formerly been assigned who had cancer. He said that recently she had called him asking that he perform her wedding ceremony. She was cured.

Although I was at the point then where I could handle the cancer, I could not handle the polyneuropathy. I could not button my own blouse or open cans or jars. The most humiliating thing was that I had to ask my husband to cut my finger- and toenails.

I tried everything that I could think of to restore feeling to my dead limbs. Nothing worked. I soaked my feet in Epsom salts, thinking that this would help. But I succeeded only in burning my feet, as I could not tell how hot the water was. My doctor cautioned me when he heard of this. I was unsteady in the shower and had to take baths. He was seriously concerned that I might step into a tub of extremely hot water and cause severe damage to my body.

More than anything else, I hated depending on people to do things for me. I was a woman in the prime of life and was finding myself with less strength than old people who were confined to nursing homes. I'm afraid that I was feeling very sorry for myself. I managed to get to Mass each week, though, and found great strength in receiving the Eucharist. As I whispered through my tears, "O Lord, I am not worthy, but only say the word and I *shall be healed,*" I knew that He was listening. Strength entered my feet, making my walk home from church always easier than the one that had brought me there.

Weeks passed since my last treatment. The numbness had now reached my knees. I was terrified. If I got worse, my family would not be able to take care of me. I didn't want them to anyway. I knew from personal experience what this does to a family.

I went to nine different doctors looking for help. I was asking to be sent for rehabilitation services. Each of them told me that there was no rehabilitation for this illness (the polyneuropathy). One of the doctors explained that usually nerve damage occurs to the fatty cells surrounding the nerve, but in my case the core of the nerves was affected. The only useful advice that I received was from a chiropractor whom I visited. He counseled me but could not help me physically. I told him of my deep faith, and he encouraged me to continue praying. He also advised me to continue to do everything that I was able to do for as long as I was able to do it. This was good advice, and although it was very difficult to follow, I did.

Among the doctors that I visited was a cancer specialist at the Cancer Research Center, in Boston. All of the doctors, including the chiropractor that I consulted, asked me if I had been able to maintain bladder and bowel control. This question terrified me. I would not have my family taking care of a person so totally dependent as that! The specialist in Boston told me that this condition occurs once in seven hundred patients who take the type of chemotherapy that I took. He told me that there were several people confined to wheelchairs for the rest of their lives as a result of this treatment and that I should consider myself "lucky" to be as well as I was. I was lucky all right. I could just barely carry my eighty-five-pound body around with the use of a cane. He also said that once the offending drugs have been removed, patients usually become no worse. But my treatment had stopped in November and the illness had progressed. It showed no indication of stopping until I, too, might be in a wheelchair. So I returned from Boston very discouraged.

I hobbled to church on Easter, my cane guiding and supporting my frail body. The only shoes that I was able to wear were some very worn-looking sneakers. I had tried to wear other shoes, but my feet would break out in sores that I could not feel although they would bleed. I was a lovely sight for the Easter parade, wearing a wig to cover my still-bald head from the eight treatments. But I didn't care. I wasn't going to church to receive admiring glances. I was going to church to receive my God, Who I knew still loved me in spite of the spectacle that I must have been.

In December, when I quit chemotherapy, the doctor had persuaded me to undergo another CAT scan. He had also recommended surgery to see if any cancer was left. If that had been so, he would have wanted me to consider either continuing treatment or starting all over again. I agreed to having both the CAT scan and surgery. While anxious to find out if the cancer was gone, I knew that I would not go back for treatment. The surgery was scheduled for January 22, 1982.

We had a local group, called the Damien Group, that was composed of cancer patients and members of their families. This group was very important to me. It functioned like group therapy. We would get together and discuss our problems and ways to deal with them collectively. Cancer is a peculiar illness, in that it is very difficult to talk about with anyone else. At least it seemed that way to me. I could discuss it with no one outside of my family, and sometimes not even with them. Among many friends that I made in this group, one was very special to me. Her name was Pat and she had been cured of ovarian cancer. Her prognosis at the time of surgery was that she had only three weeks to live unless given che-motherapy immediately. She was a lovely, vivacious woman and had been cured for a year. She and her husband were a loving couple and they attended the meeting together. At an earlier time, she had visited Father Ralph DiOrio with her brother, who was afflicted with cancer. Father had singled her out to pray for her and she was not even aware of her illness. He told her that although she would have an illness that should be attended to, she would be cured. Right after that, Pat was found to have cancer. She and I often had long conversations in which we shared our feelings. When I spoke of my impending surgery and decision to quit treatment, she recommended that I call Father DiOrio's "help line" to be prayed for on the day of my surgery. This I did and Pat prom-ised to pray for me too.

When I awoke from surgery, I was in a regular hospital room, rather than in the recovery room as I had anticipated. Soon a resident doctor came in and told me that they had found no sign of cancer. I didn't want to leave the hospital until I had heard this from the lips of my own surgeon. In fact, I would not leave until he visited me in the early evening, having just finished his last operation. He told me the good news and I readied myself to go home. Naturally, I was greatly relieved and thankful. But my excitement was watered down by the fact that I still had to deal with the polyneuropathy, which was not hidden, as the cancer had been. In fact, it had caused one of my co-workers to dub me "the little cripple."

I began thanking God every day for my cure. My doctor assured me that I was not just in remission, but that I was cured. He told me that if cancer should invade my body again it would be a totally new illness, rather than a recurrence of the cancer that had been present.

Several months later, the same doctor called to tell me that my decision to quit chemotherapy when I did had been a correct one. Through all of the experimental study of which I was a part, they had found that only six treatments are required for this type of cancer, if it responds to treatment. I was grateful that I had been part of a study that could save many people from eight needless treatments that might even cause them to develop polyneuropathy. My polyneuropathy had started in October, after just six treatments. Tears welled up in my eyes as I realized that if this knowledge had only come sooner I would be totally well.

Throughout all of this ordeal, I had become very angry with the doctors who were treating my cancer. I could not help but blame them for the difficulties that I was encountering. I argued with them and sometimes would not show up for appointments. On one occasion, I told one of the doctors who called to see if I had forgotten my appointment, that I would not visit him again until I was totally cured of the polyneuropathy. My husband was angry about my feelings toward these doctors. He said that they had done what they believed was the right thing for my illness and, after all, I was alive. But my heart was bitter. Now I can look back and realize that they were hurt by my feelings toward them and that I do love them. They are God's children and doing a very difficult job in dealing with this horrible illness. I learned a profound lesson. In order for God to forgive us, we must first forgive others.

Following my surgery, I called Pat to tell her the good news. I asked her if she had suffered the problem that I was having with my hands and feet. She said that she had to some extent but had neither required a cane nor stopped driving. Her condition had affected her handwriting and she had tired easily when walking. Once again she encouraged me to attend Father DiOrio's services in Worcester. Although I paid no attention to what she said, she gave me information as to how arrangements could be made. I did call the prayer line from time to time to pray with the volunteer.

As I became more and more depressed about the polyneuropathy, I continued to lose weight. My sister became increasingly worried and asked if she might take me to Father DiOrio's services in the hope that it might cheer me up. Although totally skeptical about what Pat had told me, she wanted to help me.

We made the trip. It was a most uplifting personal experience. I was not physically healed. But something was beginning to happen to me that I could not understand. I left there no longer feeling sorry for myself, as I had when I entered. With what I had heard, seen and felt, my depression had changed to excitement. I could not sleep all night from the exhilaration that filled my soul. My sister was probably more enthralled than I. She had gone with skepticism while I had gone with faith. My faith surprised her, I think. We stayed to the very end, lingering until the closing of the doors. This was the first of many visits that we made to these services.

On our third visit to a service, both of my sisters accompanied me. A strange thing happened. I call it miraculous. We found seats in the very front and on the center aisle, which Father DiOrio walks down when he begins to move among the people. As Father was returning down this center aisle after having prayed over many people, he stopped to bless me. I could not believe it. The moment that I had so anxiously awaited had finally come. However, when I got up on my feet I realized that I still needed my cane to aid my steps. My sisters and I left the auditorium. I sat on the steps outside and, taking the blessed oil that Father had put on my hands, rubbed it into my feet. Still I was not healed. I picked up my cane and hobbled to the car, which was parked some distance away.

At the service that day, Father had talked about the healing of many illnesses, including crippledness. His words ran through my brain over and over: "Go home now, healed, as God meant you to be healed." I thought to myself this is as far as God wants me to be healed. He wants me healed in my heart and soul only, not in my body. Little prayer leaflets had been passed out at the service. They were called "Secret to Sanctity and Happiness." It contained prayers to the Holy Spirit for each day in the week. There was a prayer at the beginning asking the Holy Spirit to show the way that He wants one to live and to accept it. I began then to pray that I might accept the affliction that I thought was to be mine for the rest of my life. But I did ask that I would not become burdensome to my family and prayed that death might take me before that could happen.

Each day as soon as I arose I said the prayer to the Holy Spirit for that particular day. The prayers asked for His guidance, strength and consolation. I asked that God make His will known. If only I would be shown the will of my Master, I promised to be submissive to everything that He permitted to happen to me.

Lo and behold the eighth day arrived, after having completed the prayers for each day of the week. It was Sunday, July 18, 1982, and a day that I shall never forget. I arose early in the morning while everyone was still asleep. It was my custom to grab furniture indoors to get from place to place, saving my cane for outdoor use. I was groggy. Starting into the living room, I forgot to grab the bureau to get me to the door knob. Then I forgot to grab the door knob to get me to the chair. Suddenly, I realized that I was walking unassisted. I could FEEL my feet on the floor. It was the first feeling that I had felt in them since October of 1981. Praise God! I WAS HEALED! Once I accepted His will, He healed me.

With the exception of the Easter Mass on Sunday, I never bothered to attend Holy Week services. Actually, I did not really appreciate how much Jesus had done for me. But this year was different. It was the most blessed and beautiful Easter season that I have ever lived through. I attended every service that was held and clung to every word that was spoken. I was most personally touched by the service on Good

Friday. This year I knew that Easter was for me personally, just as it is for you. Jesus died for us in our time just as He died for all of the generations before us and those to come. I could hardly keep a dry eye through any of the services, as my heart was so overwhelmed with gratitude. I realized that as sure as the nails went into those hands and feet, I had driven them there. As sure as He was spat upon, I had done that, too. And as sure as He was heartbroken by those sinners whom He loved the most, I was the cause of that heartbreak. I could barely contain myself, realizing this. But at the Resurrection, in spite of what I have done to Him, He opened the gates of heaven for me.

PRAYER:
Lord Jesus, what can I say to thank You for Your healing love? I hold in my hands a little prayer card that just came to me through the mail. It comes from the Association of Marian Helpers, who assist the Marian Fathers and Brothers in Stockbridge, Massachusetts. The words seem so appropriate. Yes, Lord, how true they are:

> *For every pain that we must bear*
> *For every burden, every care,*
> *There's a reason.*

> *For every grief that bows the head*
> *For every teardrop that is shed,*
> *There's a reason.*

> *For every hurt, every plight,*
> *For every lonely, pain-racked night,*
> *There's a reason.*

> *But if we trust God as we should,*
> *All must work out for our good,*
> *He . . . knows the reason!*

THANK YOU, LORD

Briea M. LaPierre

———

"OH, GOD, NOT AGAIN"

Divine strength is not usually given us until we are fully aware of our own strength.

Thomas Merton

The great apostle St. Paul gives us assurance that with faith and hope in the Risen Christ we will achieve a more perfect life. The apparent paradox, however, of human existence, being often tossed to and fro by the anguish of pain, can stifle and befog our understanding regarding the "strange ways" of the Almighty. Yet the fact remains that amid our human exile, a plethora of human suffering crowds our planet. There exist as "part and parcel" human disorders emerging in human beings. These are observed, and more so experienced by personal encounter, from a simple common cold to terminal diseases, forming as it were a huge continuum of pain. Despair, which can be fatal, nevertheless can also serve as a springboard of hope. This resurrected hope can usher a desperate soul into the riches of Divine Faith. Trust in the Divine Faith leads a person, moreover, into the Faith of Healing Prayer. Healing presupposes pain. Can one realistically ever meet such a challenge of Divine Faith over human pain? This tormenting perplexity is answered to a world in search, in some consoling degree, by Norine LaPierre and her husband, who, having once experienced the loss of an eight-week-old son, were suddenly confronted with another shockingly traumatic incident relating to a fatal illness attacking their three-month-old daughter, Briea. Little Briea was very suddenly taken ill by the disease of leukemia. Her case was diagnosed initially as a possible flu. However, testing revealed a far more serious prognosis in the diagnosis of leukemia. But very

*close friends of Mr. and Mrs. LaPierre came forth in loving
concern urging them to turn to the Almighty God, Who would
definitely console them in their grief. Moreover, they urged
the parents to present their little infant to Divine Healing
Prayer by the Apostolate of Prayer for Healing and Evangelization. Faith was activated! And both parents persisted to
present their little one to the healing touch of a priest blessed
by God. The first initial encounter with prayer was done
through the Apostolate of Prayer phone prayer line. Improvement immediately occurred! The hope that sparkled in the
parents' hearts convinced them to attend one service. That
combination of phone prayer and prayer service actualized a
complete healing. God can use anything and anyone to bring
us to the throne of His loving mercy.*

This is the story of my daughter, Briea. It all began in February of 1981, when she was three months old and seemingly
developed symptoms of the "flu." Her doctor directed me by
phone to give her half-strength formula, then water, and back
again to half-strength formula. Nothing worked! Her vomiting
and diarrhea worsened and she became extremely pale, so I
bundled her up and brought her to the doctor. After a blood
test was taken, it seemed that I waited forever to be directed
to the Emergency Room for further tests. Thinking by that
time that the doctor knew something that he was not telling
me, I broke down and cried.

We had already lost our eight-week-old son due to a heart
condition. I couldn't believe that it was all happening again!
Doctors injected her with needles all over her little body and
she screamed as my son had screamed! I tried to "block out"
the nightmare and thought aloud, "Oh, God, not again!" Finally my husband arrived. Taking him into a back room,
Briea's doctor told him to prepare himself, as her condition
was very serious and required admission into the hospital for
consultation and bone-marrow testing. The following morning, the doctors confirmed the diagnosis of Briea's illness to
be a severe form of leukemia. He informed us that her
chances of survival were only 20 percent.

Feeling absolutely desperate and knowing of nowhere else to turn, we called our neighbors for prayers. Our parish priest visited in concern and within a few days had solicited the prayers of the people of our parish and administered the sacrament of Confirmation to Briea. My whole family supported us with prayer, and then a girl who works with my husband contacted a friend of Father DiOrio's for prayer. A woman whom I did not know gave us a cross that had been blessed by him and belonged at one time to her daughter, who had been healed of leukemia. We put the cross on Briea's bed in the hospital, and the very next day she began to get better. Soon she went home, and it was two weeks early!

But our joy was short-lived. A week later, Briea reentered the hospital with a very rare case of pneumonia requiring a respirator and several tubes in her body. The doctors thought that she wouldn't live. Once again, I reached out to the last thread of hope that existed for us, the friend of Father DiOrio.

One afternoon a short while later, my husband and I came home to find the telephone ringing. It was none other than Father DiOrio's friend, who told us that while recently meeting with him she had told him about Briea. While doing so she had noticed a marked change in his expression, followed by a directive to call Briea's parents on the phone. Upon speaking with him, he asked that we put the phone on Briea's chest, but as we were not at the hospital with her this was not possible. He prayed with us, asking Jesus to use His power to heal our baby. It was hard to believe that we were talking to this man and priest who had become so well known and that all of this was happening. Improvement in Briea's condition became noticeable immediately, so we made plans to attend a healing service conducted by Father DiOrio. Understandably, the doctor did not want to release Briea from the hospital. Threatening to sign her out if he refused, it was finally agreed upon to allow her to attend.

During the healing service, Father DiOrio called out that someone was receiving a healing of leukemia. At that time, I saw Briea become flushed and warm. My first thought was one of panic that her temperature might be rising. However, as I saw her color return to normal, I realized that my baby was being healed!

Upon returning to the hospital, we told everyone the good news. In return, we received some strange looks. However, one nurse did say that she knew that Briea would be just fine.

It has now been over two years since Briea was healed, and she is doing extremely well. I truly don't think that she needs medication, but, according to the law, I have to bring her for it. I praise the Lord every day for my baby's health and tell everyone that I meet about her healing. A nurse told me that we should tattoo "MIRACLE BABY" on her forehead so that everyone might know the power of the Lord if only we ask!

It is incredible how many people have returned to the Lord through Briea since she received her healing. My own life in the Lord has been affected through her experience with the Lord. All of my decisions in life are now based on Him. My husband believes that Jesus is using her to bring His lost sheep home. People react in different ways to Briea. Last winter we took her to Disneyland, and while in a restaurant an old man looked over and said that she was a beautiful and blessed baby. Little did he know . . . or did he know?

PRAYER:
My God, my God, how can I thank You? You have spared me the anguish of the possible loss of my little child. You have healed her. Humbly I thank you. My husband and I both embrace You. We are determined to serve You to the very best of our ability in both truth and spirit. Let all praise and honor be to You for Your kindness shown to us. You have not only restored to us our child, but You have strengthened us in both mind and body. May this experience—grown from pain —ever continue on as renewed life, leading us as family to praise your name more faithfully for the rest of our lives. My newfound trust urges me to pray for the help of Your Spirit, for light and courage to be ever more faithful to our Lord

Jesus, Your Son, Who has touched our lives as our Divine Physician. O Jesus, I thank you for being there when despair knocked at our home's door. We give you gratitude for the comfort and the healing love we needed.

Ron M. Lynch

IN SEARCH OF DRINK

Jesus said to her, "Give me a drink."

John 4:7

Gilbert Keith Chesterton once described a very interesting personality in one of his essays, a Mr. Pond. In that character sketch, Chesterton stated that within each human being there resides a "monster." Is this not true, as each of us have traversed the chapters of our own autobiography? Deep within us lie those forces for both good and bad. A truly mature person is not recognized and honored by his anatomical size, huge or small; but one is honored by his/her strength of courage to say yes when yes must be said, and no when no must be spoken. But who among us can dare to judge another human person's strengths or weaknesses? There are so many influences both from within the person himself and from outside forces. A terrible influence, though in itself not evil, is alcohol—specifically through alcohol abuse. When one surrenders to these elements without reason, one depersonalizes one's whole dignity. Above all the valid means of treatment, that which is most powerful to restore the human dignity unto renewed life is the power to love *such a being. In the following story, a very good and gentle man, named Ron Lynch, huge in body but also huge in goodness, somehow became a victim of intemperate drinking. The fidelity and the never-dying love of his God, personified through the presence of a good, loyal wife, restored Ron to the status of both a remarkable gentleman and a renewed Christian.*

My name is Ron Lynch. I am forty-seven years old and married to a loving wife, Eileen. It is through her intercessory prayer and the Lord's answer to her that I am where I am today. We have four beautiful children. For twenty-five years I have been a fire fighter by profession, and I am an ex-alcoholic.

Since the age of fourteen I had a problem with drink. Of course, like a true-blue alcoholic, I would not admit to it! Being a fire fighter, I went to Mass because I feared the Lord —unless I was too hung over—or because my wife insisted that I go for the sake of the children. Most of the time it was easier to get up and go than to listen to my wife complain.

My life was reaching a point where my wife was talking about leaving me because of my drinking, and our children were emotionally upset because of our arguing. At that time I was drinking a quart of whiskey or a case of beer a day. Every chance I had to sneak a drink, I did just that. At times I even used the excuse of going to an A.A. meeting to get out of the house and then used it as an opportunity to get loaded! Once I had the first drink, I just couldn't stop until I was loaded. Then it affected my job, and the Fire Chief gave me two warnings and transferred me, telling me that if it happened again I would lose my job.

About this time we began going to St. Mary's Church, in Utica, where there was a young pastor, Father LaFache. Father announced that Father Ralph DiOrio would be coming to Utica for a healing service. My wife, who was praying very hard to keep our marriage together, involved us.

At the healing service at the Utica Auditorium on October 24, 1981, Father DiOrio said that there were four men and one woman who were being healed of alcoholism. At this time I felt a great warmth come over me and began walking toward the stage. Then Father mentioned that one of the men had a serious liver condition, and I experienced a burning sensation and shortness of breath. Although there were about six thousand people in the auditorium I just knew the Lord was calling me! All I could see was Father DiOrio standing there with a crucifix in his hands.

The next thing I knew, Father DiOrio asked me if I accepted Jesus Christ as my Lord and Saviour, and I replied that I did! Then I was slain in the Spirit, lying on my back on the stage. The most beautiful feeling, that I could never fully describe, was mine. It was one of such peace. Upon getting up, the first thing that I did was go to my wife. We embraced each other and wept. Then Father Ralph asked the married couples to renew their marriage vows. I remember thinking how beautifully the Lord works.

To this day, nineteen months later, I have neither needed nor desired a drink. And God showed me how perfect His love is in that I experienced no withdrawal symptoms. Since that day in October of 1981 I have attended daily Mass and received Communion both tearfully and joyfully, in gratitude for what God has done for me and my family. As I said before, I used to attend Mass because I feared the Lord, but now I go because I love Him.

Now that I'm walking with the Lord, I can see, through the daily reading of the Scriptures, how perfect is God's love for us. If He is so good to us on earth, imagine what it will be like spending eternity with Him in heaven. What makes it so beautiful is that it is there for all of us just for the asking.

PRAYER:
Dear Lord, here I am again. Do you remember me? I'm Ron's wife. You must remember me. Of course you do. You are God. And that's why I'm here again. Lord, I've come to complain again about Ron. Lord, he's at the bottle again. It is so sad to see, because he is running and ruining himself. And he is not really happy. And the awful thing is that he is ruining our love, and that means our home. But way down deep inside he's a good man. O God, how much I love him. Lord, before you I leave my prayer tinged with my womanly, my honest wife's tears. Please forgive me, Lord, if I cannot hold back the flood of tears. My pain is deep. Help me to intercede for the man you gave me. You gave him to me, that I might be for him a little of You loving him, even when at times he makes himself "a little boy" running from the pains of life. And so I

leave my prayer before Y O U, Lord. Will You hear me and answer me? So be it, dear Lord.

Another day, another time, I'll come back to complain again. I'll continue to complain until you make Ron right. And when you do that, dear Lord, do it for all those who, like Ron, are running, running away. Will you hear this prayer?

Thank you, Lord. . . . Thank You. . . . Thank You with all my heart. RON HAS RETURNED TO YOU. HE'S HEALED!

Frank McMurray

———————

NOTHING LESS THAN A
MIRACLE

If a man will begin with certainties, he shall end in doubts: but if he will be content to begin with doubts, he shall end in certainties.

Francis Bacon

In a recent pilgrimage visit to Lourdes, Pope John Paul II was frequently seen placing his hand on the faces and foreheads of many sick pilgrims whom he met at that sacred, blessed grotto of Our Lady of Lourdes, France. He was quoted as having stated that many present at that grotto could definitely witness to the fact that trial could produce through faith a rebirth; *and moreover,* that the sick must not be defeated by their afflictions. *Is it not true that throughout life unexpected tragedies just about disarm us? Such catastrophes have the power of casting one into deep doubt—to be uncertain, to live in a questionable state, anguished to such a degree that one would just about cross the barrier of despair. Tragedy, however, has a way of bringing us into ourselves. We can muster strengths into realms of behavior far surpassing the normal pattern of thinking. In the case presentation of Frank McMurray, that which survived him into the graces of a loving Miracle-God was his undaunted faith that the God he knew was a God whose promises are life unto those that find them, and health to all their flesh (Proverbs 4:22). Overcoming the tragedy that struck Frank McMurray was truly a miracle beyond any human explanation. Once before, way back there in his life, Frank had known that God announced Himself to be the Healer of His people with these words: "I am the Lord that healeth thee" (Exodus 15:26). The faith that this man had in his God could find no doubt in God. The only doubt that brought fear to Frank was that his doubts about*

*doubts could devilishly influence him. So if he had to doubt
something, he was going to doubt his doubts, because they
are unreliable. His belief, his extraordinary faith in God,
proved to him and to us who witness his story that one of the
most wonderful statements about Jesus is that "Jesus Christ
is the same yesterday, and today, and forever" (Hebrews
13:8). This Jesus is the Christ who walked the shores of Galilee, who preached and taught, who healed the sick, cleansed
the lepers, raised the dead, made the deaf hear, and* Who
made the lame walk! *May this simple narration serve you,
the reader, as an anchor for real, vital faith. May it convince
you to act upon God's promises of health, which not only
include restoration for the soul and spirit, but include also
that of the body. May all hearts, humble and sincere, of the
"poor in spirit," who make up the masses of our humanity, be
blessed as God would bless them through the power of His
Word.*

Five years ago I was struck by a car while living in Califor-
nia. My ear was ripped off in the accident and five ribs were
broken. I also sustained a compound fracture of my left leg,
and my right ankle was badly cut.

The doctor wanted to amputate my leg because of the severity of the compound fracture. Instead, however, I underwent three major operations involving two bone transplants.
I was in the hospital over a year. For six months of that time I
had three rods through my leg. This was not successful, so
they tried a new method. The doctor put six rods through the
bones to hold them in place until they healed, and this was
extremely painful. He told me that I would have to wear a
brace and walk with a cane for the rest of my life. Then I
returned to Connecticut, remaining under the treatment of a
physician.

A year prior to my accident I had attended three of Father
DiOrio's healing services and been cured of painful arthritis.
So I decided to attend another service. On January 24, 1980, I
sat in the rear of the church. There was a large crowd that
day. Suddenly I heard Father DiOrio tell the people that

while in prayer that morning he had seen a man with a leg brace who was wearing a brown boot and black rubbers. He asked that the man in the church who fit that description come to the altar. Knowing that it was myself, I went up to the "Healing Priest" in the front of the church. He asked me a few questions and then prayed with me. I was slain in the Spirit. When I came to, Father asked me if I felt the urge to remove my brace and run through the church. I did just that.

Since that remarkable day, I have had no need for a leg brace and I walk without a cane. The pain pills that I had to take both day and night are no longer a part of my life and I have no further need for sleeping pills. After the service, an X ray showed that my leg had been healed. I know that it is the work of God!

PRAYER:
Dear God, the miracle of my life is that I can walk again when all walking was stated as hopeless. But Your words were in my heart and on my lips. And they were as effective as when You said, "Let there be light" (Genesis 1:3). Your words were effective even in that moment of history when even in the face of the humanly impossible, the holy chosen virgin believed in your words, and from her came forth your dear Son, our Saviour and our Healer. O God, how true it is that there can never be failure when we adhere to Your promise; Your voice speaking through Your promise excludes all reason for doubt. Thank You so much for giving me a lively faith, a vital faith that finds its seed in Your own proclamation: "I am the Lord that healeth thee" (Exodus 15:26).

"Doc" *Everett A. Rivers*

———

ONCE I FORGOT MYSELF, YOU, O LORD, REMEMBERED ME

Now, which of these is easier: to say, "Your sins are forgiven," or to say, "Get up and walk"?

Matthew 9:5

Discovery has always been exciting, because it bears within itself a spirit of adventure. The object of discovery is always to some degree—small or large—a "voyage." The greatest discovery is when a person travels along life's way, groping at times for a feeling of security or for a guiding light. Sometimes men and women are so enraptured in the business of search that they do not zero in on the real. Sometimes a person needs to lie down upon a bed of pain. In so doing, being confined by sickness and disease, one is able to look up to the heavens to Him Who from all eternity continuously speaks to us mortals, by circumstances and created beings, about who we are, where we are going, and Who our God is. Maybe this is the only way God can send us sufficient grace to save our lives, to put this earth's quests into objective focus, and to be enlightened as to their use for our inevitable eternity. The story of Everett A. Rivers, who has always been known by the nickname "Doc" Rivers, is such a story.

For seven years, "Doc" was the victim of multiple sclerosis. This is a chronic, slowly progressive disease of the central nervous system. It is characterized by scattered hardened patches of destroyed nerve tissue in both the brain and the spinal cord. This illness results in multiple neurological signs and symptoms. Its prognosis is debilitation, although the victim's life span is not decreased. The illness, however, progresses rapidly. It is interesting to read how "Doc" speaks of the manner in which the good Lord, his God, calls him to a renewed life of God's important presence. In such an experience, God's touch of new life arouses within this man a new message of faith, hope and love. The Spirit fell upon Everett, the "Doc." His whole life erupted afresh, and love overflowed. And in that moment of truth, a new Jesus appeared as Inviter, welcoming another disciple. Jesus called Doc Rivers from his bed of pain, and He showed Everett how much He needs him in His new economy of loving mankind.

October 2, 1980, seemed like any other day. The only exception was that we had planned a trip to Worcester, Massachusetts, to see a priest who a friend claimed had "healing powers."

For seven years I had been unable to work, due to multiple sclerosis. Atrophy had developed from my waist down, and the last year or so I had become confined to a wheelchair. In addition, seizures were a problem for me and I was recovering from recent abdominal surgery. To be truthful, I had reached a point where I could not do a great deal for myself and really no longer cared.

I was not one that would have been considered a religious person. My religious practices might have been more easily described as those of an on-again-off-again Catholic. I knew nothing of salvation, and Who God really was and how I was to show love for Him were unclear to me.

On one previous occasion, in July of 1980, I had seen Father DiOrio, in Glens Falls, New York. Leaving the service on that day, I felt uplifted in a way that I could not quite explain. All I knew was that something seemed to have happened to me spiritually. But I still could not walk. However, after that I did begin going to church, and this was something that I had not done in a long time.

It was after Mass on a Sunday when my friend approached me with an invitation to take a trip to see the Healing Priest. Although I responded that I really did not need to see him again, I decided to go anyway. So, on October 2, I all but crawled onto the bus. All of the people were singing and

praying—just like something out of an evangelistic movie—
and I didn't quite know what to make of it.

Upon arrival at St. John's Church, in Worcester, I was in
awe at seeing the number of people attending the service.
While waiting outside of the church I began to feel somewhat
strange. My attention turned to the afflicted people around
me, and suddenly my problem no longer seemed to matter. I
found myself praying in a different manner than ever before.
Although much time has now passed, I still remember some
of those people well. There was a woman without knee caps
and a mother holding a child who was unable to function in
any way on his own. I began asking God to help these people,
because they seemed to really believe that He could help
them.

As the line began moving into the church, in desperation
people pushed in an attempt to get closer to the front. I recall
being a little frightened and telling an usher at the door that
someone else could take my place. Assuring me that everything would be all right, he proceeded to pick up my chair
with two other men and carry me up to the front of the
church.

There were people everywhere, and a beautiful voice was
singing the "Ave Maria." A boy next to me was slain in the
Spirit. I began shaking, and bent over in my chair to see if I
could assist him. To my surprise, I shook even more, slumped
over and became very warm. A good friend was sitting next
to me and I remember him reaching out to me and quietly
saying, "Praise Jesus." At that very moment I got out of my
wheelchair and walked! Father had called for the person who
was healed of multiple sclerosis to come forth, and I was
shaking, crying and walking forward. Somewhat confused
and yet ever so happy, I walked to the center of the church.
Father kept on praying with the congregation. He did not
touch me. A man without legs reached for my hand and I felt
something beautiful happen. It was something that I cannot
explain. At the end of the service an usher approached me
and said, "This is only the beginning. Many won't believe it,
but stand on your faith!"

Since that October 2, my life has not been the same. I have

neither returned to a wheelchair nor required medication. In fact, I've gone back to work and am presently managing a small business.

My spiritual life has brought me great joy. Every day, I study and meditate on Scripture and have learned to pray before beginning each new venture. I've become actively involved with young people in my community and in my church, where I hope to be a deacon someday. Countless opportunities have arisen for me to share the Word and witness to others.

However, although the Lord has affirmed me in many ways, each one seemingly more beautiful than the one before, He has tested me too. But, each time, I find myself increasingly more grateful for the gift of faith that allows me to believe with Paul that "The trials that you have had to bear are no more than people normally have. You can trust God not to let you be tried beyond your strength, and with any trial he will give you a way out of it and the strength to bear it" (1 Corinthians 10:13). Paul also tells us: "And for anyone who is in Christ, there is a new creation; the old creation has gone, and now the new one is here" (2 Corinthians 5:17). I know that I have been born anew!

PRAYER:
Lord, as I kneel before You, my heart rises in prayer. I cannot help but to recall those words which I read somewhere among my past readings: "So panteth my soul after thee, O God." I wish I could remember where they came from, but I don't at this moment. Yet they speak of my longing for the "best" in life. I have sought and searched. But along that way of quest, You halted me to stop and rest awhile. You wanted to speak to me. You gave me time through my human condition of illness. O God, I would not be here today, where I am, if it had not been for Your love. O God, I do remember some great quotation of my past readings. I feel somewhat proud— if I may say so myself—that I do remember some great author. It comes from the renowned Plato. May I say it to You, Lord? I know You know it already, but I just have to say it. It

applies so much to me. It describes me so well. Here it is, Lord.

> The desire and the pursuit of the whole is called
> love.   Plato

Thank You, Lord; this is my story!

Carol Scacco

———————

A CHILD IS BORN

Every time a child is born it shows that God has not lost faith in human nature!

Rabindranath Tagore
(Indian poet)

One of God's finest gifts to women is the gift of a baby. What a divine gift that is! There is such a splendid mystery in that act of creation! In the situation of Carol Scacco, of Pennsylvania, this particular joy, this awesome responsibility of bringing forth God's creation, the joy and the pleasure of nurturing a new person, almost was not to be. Carol was threatened by the news of carrying a baby in breech position. To Carol, bringing forth this new life was anxiously awaited with joy beyond articulation. However, intruding upon this joy of ushering forth new life was the knowledge that her fetus rested in abnormal status. Such a complication raises the question not only of an unusually difficult and painful delivery, but it also might present a menace to the survival of the infant. But the amazing and incredible fact of Carol's story is that God became the obstetrician. *His Divine Physician's hand miraculously reversed the position of the infant dwelling within the womb. But the remarkable point of interest is that God did this through the process of healing prayer over the medium of the radio program "The Hour of Healing with Father Ralph A. DiOrio," Station WORC (Worcester, Massachusetts), in 1980. As you read this narration, we hope you enjoy what God can do.*

I was forty-six years old when I became pregnant in 1980. To have a baby that late in life concerned me. Isn't it common knowledge that there is a risk involved in late pregnancy? I had heard before that the chances of retardation occurring in a child are far greater when the mother is over forty. And then, too, I would not be a young mother as my little one grew up. All of these thoughts crossed my mind when I was told that there was new life within me. Later, the doctors confirmed that it would be a breech delivery.

When my expected date of giving birth was drawing near, I called Father Ralph DiOrio during his radio program. For a few hours on Wednesday evenings the "Hour of Healing" was broadcast, and I knew that Father accepted calls from people in need. I told him that my baby had been lying in breech position throughout the whole time of my pregnancy and that I had only one more prenatal visit to go. Father asked me to place my hand on my stomach, and proceeded to pray with me over the phone.

Two days went by and I felt nothing unusual happening. Friday night came, and after taking a shower I settled comfortably on our couch. Suddenly I felt a terrible pain in my stomach, causing tears to stream down my face. My husband thought that I had gone into labor. I insisted that this was not true, although I had only three weeks left until delivery.

Then we looked in awe! We could actually see that the baby had made an outline on my stomach. My pain eased and I relaxed again, knowing that everything would be all right.

A week later, I returned to my doctor. He was amazed to see that the baby had turned, and wondered how it had happened.

After seven hours of easy labor my baby was born naturally. I knew tremendous joy and contentment, for is anything impossible with God?

PRAYER:
Dearest Lord, please continue to make me conscientious to the grace that You gave me in allowing me to bear my child under Your divine hand. Give me a grateful heart so that all the days You give me to live, I may live these days for caring

for my child in the way You will. Just enable me to be the kind of mother who will please You as I seek to please the needs of this little one. What a holy trust You have given me by the gift of this child! Let me not falter in raising my child in Your holy tender fear, in Your honorable favor.

Danielle Snyder

———

THE CHILD WHO EATS
EVERYTHING

Nothing therefore can come between us and the love of Christ, even if we are troubled or worried, or being persecuted, or lacking food or clothes, or being threatened or even attacked. . . . These are the trials through which we triumph, by the power of him who loved us.

Romans 8:35–37

A mother's heart suffers with her child, for she is the heart of the family. A father's love is tormented by doubt at the unanswerable questions to the problem of pain, especially when that pain strikes a member of his own family. Faith alone in a God of love and concern is a powerful force to conquer that which is apparently unanswerable and impossible. And so is the story of the parents of little Danielle Snyder, seven at the time of her healing, in 1981. Presently she lives as happily as any child and eats as well as any growing child. Why speak of her eating? Because little Danielle suffered with severe allergies pertaining to the intake of a variety of foods. The term "allergy" denotes an altered tissue reaction to one or more substances. The development of allergic manifestations depends partly upon inheritance. Although all persons are potentially allergic, susceptibility to allergy varies. About 75 percent of allergic children have a family history of allergy. An allergy to a substance cannot be cured. It may only be kept sufficiently under control so that no symptoms are produced. In the case of Danielle, terrible symptoms were present. Some of these were bleeding rashes, severe urinary burning, confusion of mental outlook, accompanied with hyperactivity. In 1981, Mr. and Mrs. Snyder flew from Kansas City, Missouri, to one of our healing services. At that service, God consoled the parents first. All around them, they witnessed many other parents with their sick children, with conditions of illness far surpassing that of Danielle. The par-

*ents' hearts and minds were touched. When they saw the
other parents and the other children, they forgot their own
problem with Danielle. Immediately changing their attitude,
they suddenly found themselves praying for the other children. And at that unselfish moment, God touched the child of
their own life. And little Danielle spent five hours in peace
and tranquillity. She appeared totally out of character, with
absolutely no hyperactivity being demonstrated. That service brought healing love to both parents and child.*

Danielle's ninth birthday is today. She's happy, pretty and
healthy. This has not always been the case. The first seven
and one half years of her life were spent with severe allergies, so much so that they affected every aspect of her being,
including her behavior and thought processes, as well as
physical symptoms.

From birth, Danielle was like a jet plane traveling at super-
sonic speed. As an infant, she didn't sleep well. The doctor
said she had colic. As an older child, she still stayed up very
late. Rather than walking, she always ran. She touched everything in sight before I could stop her. She never obeyed
well, as she seemed too busy to listen. I even had her hearing
checked, because she didn't speak clearly. She heard fine, but
spoke so fast the words ran together. She had always been
extremely capable for her age, so I was not concerned about
her ability to learn. The problem was that I was wearing out.

I was expecting my third child when Danielle was three,
and I realized that I had to get her under control. During a
spanking one day, she said, "Mommy, why are you being so
mean to me?" At that point I saw that she had drawn no
connection between the crime and the punishment. I stopped
punishing her, since she was not aware that she had a behavioral problem. Her doctor suggested a complete neurological
study, which I feared lest the recommendation of drugs be
made as a solution to her problem.

Having heard of the Feingold Diet to help hyperactive children, I mentioned to the doctor that I would like to try it on
Danielle. After doing a considerable amount of research and

reading, it was clear to me, because of the fluctuation in her degree of agitation, that she suffered from minimal brain dysfunction due to some outside stimuli. I put her on a diet that excluded all artificial colors, flavors, preservatives, foods that she could not tolerate and those that were medically known to be highly allergenic. Within four and a half days my three-and-a-half-year-old child became another person. She was calm and kind and acted like a normal child. I tested the diet over and over again, and each time she went off the diet the old symptoms quickly reappeared. All of her food had to be pure and properly prepared. If her diet was broken, she would experience rashes that would bleed, urinary burning that would cause her to scream with pain, confusion, or hyperactivity. On one occasion she ate at McDonald's and almost died of an asthmatic attack, although she had never had asthma before. For five years she was on this strict diet, and my husband and I spent most of our time in the kitchen cooking everything for her from natural foods. When traveling, we took a small cooler with her food in it. As time went on she carried her own food to parties, Disneyland and everywhere she went. She was totally cooperative, telling us that her mind got confused when she ate "junk" food.

Although we are members of Pine Ridge Presbyterian Church, Danielle attends St. Therese Catholic Elementary School, as we prefer that she has an early Christian education. Her year in kindergarten and the beginning of her year in first grade were uneventful when she stayed on her diet. However, when she accidentally ate the wrong food, she even wrote letters reversed. She was in the top of her class until, for no apparent reason, she began to become allergic to foods that she had previously tolerated. Her teacher told us that she learned with increasing difficulty, and she went from the first reading group to the last. And she looked poorly.

We started eliminating foods one by one. The children at school teased her about her diet, and she cried, thinking that she could never be like them. This, along with the time and expense of shopping for her special foods all over the Kansas City area, ordering foods by mail, the special preparation of every meal (inclusive of candy and medication such as lip balm prepared from beeswax melted on the stove), and the monitoring of her environment against such things as lawn spray finally caused me to reach my breaking point. Finally, in desperation, I began praying for help.

Two weeks later, I saw Father DiOrio on television and had a strong desire to take Danielle to him. My husband agreed, and we made arrangements to travel from Kansas City, Missouri, to Worcester, Massachusetts.

Being Presbyterians, we were not quite sure what to expect in regard to a healing service of this nature. I had always believed in divine healing but thought it happened to only a few, and far between. In all honesty I was also leery of the charismatic movement. I truly felt that we would be blessed by attending. Possibly we would find a new doctor or maybe I would simply gain more patience to cope with the problem. I really didn't know what to expect.

When the date finally arrived, we flew to Boston with Danielle's cooler of special food in hand and rented a car to drive to Worcester. So far from home, I was amazed to meet a lady in the line from Kansas City who was the aunt of one of Danielle's classmates. Once seated in the audience, we discovered that the little girl who was seated directly in front of our Danielle was also named Danielle. This truly unnerved me. My husband and I quickly noticed that we were surrounded by many children who had fatal and serious diseases, and we felt blessed. After all, our Danielle wasn't near death. We both began to pray for the people around us. For nearly five hours we were in those seats and Danielle neither complained nor became difficult to handle. She had always had a unique understanding of Christianity, but this was totally out of character for her in her agitated state.

After the service, we all felt peaceful. Driving back to Boston, we stopped for dinner. I got Danielle's cooler out of the car and my husband said, "Is that all the stronger your faith is?" So I put the cooler back in the car. Danielle ordered what she wanted from the menu. Having a 7-Up to drink brought a light to her little face. For years she had exhibited a self-discipline that most adults don't have.

From that meal forward she has been eating normally, partaking of foods from the grocery store and eating "junk" candy just like all the other kids. She has been eating in restaurants and candy stores and anywhere and everywhere that a little girl would want. I almost couldn't believe it, but that was July 26, 1981, and today she is still perfectly fine. At first I was almost afraid to accept it as fact, but my husband, my parents (who live next door), my sister and my neighbor all speak of how peaceful she is now. Her marks in the second grade were all A's and B's and her teacher says she's a "smart cookie."

It's as real as my blond, blue-eyed healthy daughter of nine. She knows that Jesus has healed her and tells me not to cry when we speak about it, but being the recipients of such grace will for a lifetime humble me to tears.

PRAYER:

Lord, we are simple parents. We try so hard to be just as beautiful as You would expect from parents. We love You so much! And we take seriously those gifts You give to us in this life. We thank You for our little children. But our little Danielle was not too well. She suffered so much anguish with allergies. Our hearts ached. What could we do to bring restoration to this little "bundle of joy" You shared with us in this life? Oh, how a parent's heart suffers! We thought for a moment of time only of little Danielle. We forgot the pains of others. But then, dear Lord, You reminded us that original sin has touched mankind as a whole. And during that service of peace and love, of hope and healing, our faith made us "big." We stopped for a while to place our minds in holy empathy to the cries of other human parents. Oh, God, how they, too, were suffering; yes, suffering even far greater anguish than we! And so we prayed, and pray we still for all of Your children. You heard our prayer for others when we forgot ourselves. And in hearing our "unselfish prayer," at that moment, You did not forget to heal our little Danielle. THANK YOU, LORD.

Connie Spadell

———◆———

"LITTLE HEALINGS COUNT TOO!"

Give, and there will be gifts for you: a full measure, pressed down, shaken together, and running over, will be poured into your lap; because the amount you measure out is the amount you will be given back.

Luke 6:38

The following story is one in which a gentle woman, gracious and outgoing, received from the Almighty Father a healing from cancer of the breast. The media of healing were both from the channels of healing prayer and from the medical profession—one leading to the other. Mrs. Connie Spadell is a woman whose life consists in giving to others and seeking no return. She is a giver, not a taker. God blessed that spirit through His own reward as He graced her with the healing love and the healing restoration of His Sacred Heart.

I've told and retold my story, or bits of my story, many times, but this is my first attempt to put it on paper. And I'm finding it a difficult task, for it is really a composite of several small stories. Because each one contributes to the "whole," if I am to get across the inner feelings, the depth of emotion experienced, then I must skip no detail. Please bear with me.

Emotional pain for me has always been more devastating, more difficult to bear, than physical pain. I had often wondered how I'd feel, how I'd react, if someone really close to me died. On Friday night, August 28, 1981, I found out.

As I was preparing to retire, I received a telephone call from my brother, who said simply and swiftly, "Mom's gone. You'd better come." I was shocked and numb. His words had registered but had not fully sunk in. How could this be? Mom was going to be sixty-four in just a few days. My sisters and I were planning a birthday celebration.

Quickly, I packed an overnight bag and, with my husband, my two sisters and their husbands, made the eighty-mile trip to our parents' home. We cried most of the way, taking time out only to pray the rosary. The hospital where Mom was taken after she collapsed had agreed to hold the body there so that we could pay our final respects before they turned it over to Temple University. Against my wishes (my father and sister had given in to my mother's pleadings and had signed their approval), my mother had donated her body to science in the hope that someone, somewhere, would benefit and perhaps be spared some of the crippling and agonizing pain that accompanied the rare form of arthritis with which she was afflicted.

The night passed in an emotional medley of tears, talk and the usual guilt-ridden and angry questions. "Why couldn't they do something?" "Why didn't I call her today?" "Why didn't I do more for her, and more often?" Endless questions . . . endless prayers . . . endless doubts . . . endless night!

In the early-morning hours, eyes swollen and hearts aching, our forlorn little group arrived at the hospital. A nurse gently led us into the morgue, where a body lay covered with a sheet. My first thought was "That can't be Mom! That body looks pregnant!" But, oh, God! It *was* Mom, swollen with body fluids, waxen and cold, but yet somehow peaceful. Can you imagine what it does to your insides, to your heart, to have to say good-bye to the dearest of mothers under those sterile, cold, antiseptic and unfeeling conditions? As the nurse handed me a small, blue plastic bag marked "Patient's belongings," I knew then the full meaning of the description "grief-stricken."

Back home at Dad's once again, our tired minds wondered what to do next. Sitting on Mom's bed, still turned down from where she had slept, I touched her pillow and looked about her room. On her nightstand, along with her rosaries, was a small holy-card. As I read the prayer on the back, I noted the name, Rev. Ralph A. DiOrio, printed on the bottom. This was the priest Mom had written to and whom she so desperately had wanted to see. She had mentioned him to us more than once and said that he was her only hope to be healed. On her desk, with little red check marks near two future dates, I found Father DiOrio's schedule of crusades for 1981. Her arthritis had been so severe that it limited the amount of time she could spend sitting in a car, and even a trip to visit us often resulted in an increase of pain and discomfort for several days.

But she had had such faith in this priest! I wished, then and there, with all my heart, that we had somehow been able to arrange a trip to one of these healing sessions. My mother was a convert, but she was a most devout Catholic. It was comforting to know that she had gone to confession and received the Holy Eucharist just a few days before her sudden death.

In life, she had often commented, "I want no flowers when I die, no fancy funeral. I only want prayers and Masses." And so it would be. Several telephone calls were made and we finally arranged to have a funeral Mass said on Monday, August 31, to be followed by a breakfast for our large family and friends at a local restaurant. Somehow we all got through that long, bleak weekend, and finally Monday arrived.

Facing everyone at the Mass at our home parish and receiving condolences only added to my grief. I just could not stop the tears. After Mass, my cousin Elaine took my hand, saying she could not stay for the breakfast because her husband was flying in a few friends for dinner, and that if one of the guests wasn't Father DiOrio, she wouldn't mind, but as it was, she really was needed at home. I looked at her, and slowly it registered. "Father WHO?" I asked. "Father DiOrio," she said. I just couldn't believe my ears! Oh, the irony of it all! I quickly told her that it had been Mom's dearest dream in life to see him, and here he would be in town today, actually in Pennsylvania, the day of her funeral Mass! "When the breakfast is over, why don't you and your sisters come to my home and meet Father?" she asked. Quickly we agreed.

Later that afternoon, after the last guest had gone, we drove the short distance to my cousin's lovely, country home. Many other people were already there. In fact, it was crowded and I thought that perhaps we should leave. But we didn't. Shortly after we arrived, Elaine introduced us to a tiny, sparkling woman named Molly, who turned out to be Molly DiOrio, Father's mother. Just about then, two priests walked into the room. Looking across the crowd at the one, I thought, "He's not Father DiOrio. I know him." But suddenly he began blessing people—and it *was* him! Quietly I watched. He showed such warmth and concern as he moved from person to person! Elaine prompted us to go receive his blessing, but I declined. There were so many people there—sick and crippled people—who came with such hope, and who really needed his blessing—that I felt foolish. Besides, only nineteen months before, God had indeed blessed me, I felt. In January 1980 I survived surgery for a massive blood clot on the brain, with positively no aftereffects. (That is a separate story and not relevant here.) And daily I counted my blessings!

But Molly insisted, "You three women just lost your mother. Father will bless you." And she led us, tear-stained and heavy-hearted, through the people to him. Not knowing what to expect, I watched as he first blessed my sister Loretta. And then it was my turn. I nervously murmured something like, "I had an operation on my head but I'm really fine—but I just lost my mother." And as I looked at this gentle face, his fingers reached out to the *exact* spot where the hole was left in my skull. How did he know it was *there?* He touched it and then anointed my forehead. And that was the last thing I remember.

I don't know how long I lay there. I heard nothing, felt nothing, saw nothing. What *did* I experience? Oh! So often I've tried to recapture those moments in time, and how often I've tried to put the feeling into words. "Peace," "joy," "quiet" —these are only words, words created by man. Somehow it seems as if there are no appropriate, applicable words in our language to do justice to a description. The closest I have been able to come is this: "Hope fulfilled." Think about that. The thoughts provoked can be endless.

Opening my eyes to the unfamiliar surroundings, I saw Father kneeling at my side, his hand holding my own. I felt only semiconscious. "Don't make me come back. Let me stay," I whispered. At first I didn't remember saying those words until Father repeated them to me. Looking into his eyes, I saw my grief and sorrow mirrored there; and I saw, too, the pains, the anguish, the doubts, the sufferings of all those to whom he ministered. Here was a priest who should have been a total stranger, and yet I felt I knew all about him and the heavy burden he bore with such silent strength and patience. Silently, I promised myself I'd pray for him.

The rest of that day is still dreamlike in my mind. I felt that only half of me was on earth, watching a scene of events happening to someone else, while the other half was calm, even joyous, though detached. Later that afternoon, Father said a beautiful, outdoor Mass and he called upon me and my sisters to read. The memory of that Mass, the breeze gently touching our faces, Father's soft words, the beauty of the mountains in the distance, is one I'll always cherish.

Before we left, we asked for, and received, Father's address. I promised I'd write. And I did. A few days later, I penned a short note of gratitude to him and Molly. And so began our friendship.

It wasn't until much later that I realized I'd experienced an emotional healing. I had worried about how I would return to work without breaking down as I faced the kindness and sympathy of my co-workers. But after being blessed by Father, I found the tears were gone. I cried no more. Where there had been grief and that burdening sorrow, there now was just a peaceful sort of sadness, and I *knew* I'd be all right. I was actually able to return to work the very next day! People were amazed to have me greet them with a calm exterior and an inner glow instead of the expected tears; and it seemed that everyone—but me—knew that something special had happened!

I was curious about this Father DiOrio. I read his book, listened to some borrowed tapes of his radio programs and continued to correspond with him. After a few months, I had the opportunity of attending one of Father's retreats. It was my first, and I enjoyed it immensely. But I hungered to know more about this new and loving Jesus, Whom Father spoke of

with such conviction. From the days of my early parochial
schooling, I had viewed Jesus as good and kind and merciful,
but also as a sort of stern father figure. This "new" Jesus was
not to be feared but loved!

Five months passed, and again I found myself on the bus
heading for Massachusetts and another retreat. It was March.
It was cold. But my soul was warm with expectation of all
that was to come. And my soul was not disappointed. What a
retreat! Because it was Lent, Father based his retreat on the
Passion, the suffering of Jesus. As long as I live, I will never
forget the Saturday-evening session, when he invited us to
come to the sacristy and prostrate ourselves, if we so chose,
before the Blessed Sacrament while he retold the "Way of the
Cross." If I close my eyes, even now, I can feel the roughness
of the carpet on my cheek, the dampness of my tears and the
sweet pressure of Aline's hand in mine as we lay there, listening to his divinely inspired words. (Aline is one of Father's
devoted workers; we had gone to the altar together.) If ever I
had doubted Father DiOrio's abilities or the power of his gifts
received from the Holy Spirit, the doubts were forever removed that night. I still firmly believe that Father's greatest
gift is not his healing power but his ability to teach, preach
and lead the listener to know and love our Saviour, Jesus
Christ.

That retreat provided an intense soul-searching and such a
beautiful inward journey that it led me to new insights and
greater understanding regarding my own life and the lives of
others. I found certain priorities totally rearranged! Emotionally, I felt emptied and drained, while, at the same time, renewed and refreshed. That's a contradiction, isn't it? It is not
easy to explain. Where there *had* been emptiness, there now
was an overwhelming, overflowing love for the crucified
Jesus, His Sacred Heart and His Holy Mother, Mary.

Poor, dear, beloved Mary! To me she will always be Christianity's first martyr. Jesus' Passion ended with His crucifixion and death, but Mary's crucifixion continued for years as
she relived every vivid, painful detail over and over and over
in her mind. I wonder how many nights she wakened, gripped
with horror and drenched with sweat as the nightmare re-

curred? What an awesome, unbelievable burden for any mother's heart to bear!

That retreat in March was also to provide an even greater reward. As part of his theme on the topic of "Holistic Healing," Father DiOrio had arranged to have several guest speakers. A nutritionist spoke on the association of proper diet to good health, and Dr. Scott, a retired gynecologist and author of the book *Woman, Know Thyself,* spoke on female-related matters. He particularly stressed the importance of estrogen after menopause and suggested women ask for an estrogen count at the time of their Pap tests. I enjoyed the speakers, but because of the retreat's impact on my spiritual life, that portion of the weekend seemed a poor second. But the Holy Spirit obviously was working. . . .

A few weeks after I returned home, a nagging voice kept prompting me to schedule an appointment for a checkup and a Pap test. I was overdue; and early in May, I finally did. Following Dr. Scott's suggestion, I requested an estrogen count. My Pap test turned out fine, but I was definitely estrogen-deficient. Before any replacement therapy could be initiated, my doctor requested that I have a routine mammogram. (I'd had no lump in either breast.) Two days after the test, I received a call from the doctor's office. "Doctor would like to see you to discuss your mammogram." I knew if it had been okay, they would have just given me the results over the phone. But I refused to panic and arranged to go in the next day. Sure enough, the mammogram showed the distinct possibility of cancer in the right breast. Infiltrating intraductal carcinoma—a biopsy was now needed.

The following Tuesday, I was admitted and scheduled for surgery. I agreed to a biopsy only. I did not want any quick decisions made to do extensive surgery while I was under general anesthesia. "One thing at a time," I told myself. The tissue was sent away for further diagnosis, and Friday I was sent home. Waiting was the hard part. The weekend dragged on. Monday afternoon, I went into the doctor's office to have the incision checked. One look at his face and I had my answer. "Your test was positive," he said. "With this type of cancer, surgery is our only recommendation. You will need a modified radical mastectomy, followed perhaps by radiation, chemotherapy or both." Somehow I wasn't surprised. I had expected the verdict and was prepared.

I requested that an appointment be made at Geisinger Hospital, the large facility where my neurosurgery had been performed, for a consultation and a second opinion. And this is where I can shorten my story. The second opinions confirmed the initial diagnosis. Surgery was performed and my recovery was rapid. Best of all, because the cancer was discovered at such an early stage, no additional treatment was required. I continue to be monitored, and will be for several years. But deep in my heart, I *know* it's gone for good!

Looking back over the past year, I see how richly blessed I was. Because of the early discovery of my cancer? Yes! But more so because I was able to weather the entire ordeal without fear, undue anxiety or excessive emotional upheaval. That, in itself, made it so much less a burden on my husband and daughters. I am grateful to Jesus. I am grateful to Father Ralph.

There is much more that could be said, but I feel guilty taking up even this much space with my simple story. It certainly isn't a spectacular tale. I almost wish I *did* have a grand story to tell of a healing, one that would leave a permanent imprint on the reader's memory. But I guess, after all, little miracles, little healings, little simple stories do count too. God chooses to touch our lives in many different ways. Emotional healing . . . spiritual rebirth . . . physical health . . . holistic healing . . . just *eight words?* Not to this lady.

PRAYER:
My dearest Jesus, in Your divine wisdom, You choose so many different ways to touch our lives and bring us close to You. Sometimes You use sickness, heartache and pain. On occasion You will even call home to heaven one of our loved ones. For it is during these dark moments that Your divine presence is most keenly felt.

I thank You, Lord Jesus, for my sorrows and sufferings. I thank You for touching my life so beautifully through your dedicated servant and priest Father Ralph DiOrio. Most of all I thank You for allowing my soul to blossom and grow with love for You and Your suffering Sacred Heart. I choose to ask no other grace than to continue in that growth, until all that shall remain of me is total and perfect love for You. For in the final analysis, for all mankind, love is all that will remain. Perhaps, sweet Jesus, these simple words of mine will best explain:

"When my earthly life is over, and when I'm laid to rest, I'd like it said that 'loving' is what I did the best."

Mary Ann Spinoso

———◆———

THE WOMAN WITH THE
ONYX RING

I thank you with all my heart, Lord my God,
. . . your love for me has been so great.

Psalm 86:12–13

Many times in life, God asks us, through the various incidents befalling us, to be more than conquerors. So very often each one of us must believe beyond doubt that God really wills that we be conquerors. He aids us by allowing us his grace to trust him, to believe in his promises. Mary Ann Spinoso is exemplary of such a relationship with her God. A year before coming to our healing service, Mary Ann became ill with lupus. Very often Mary Ann suffered painful arthritis, fatigue, and loss of her hair. Skin rashes were also apparent. Lupus is a chronic and often fatal systemic disease. It is characterized by changes in the vascular system. A butterfly pattern of skin rash is frequently seen, spreading across the bridge of the nose. Other marked symptoms include fever, arthritis, and signs of kidney, lung and heart involvement in varying degrees. The cause is unknown. It occurs most often in women.

On July 10, 1982, I attended a healing service with my family in Worcester, Massachusetts. It was such a beautiful service. Father DiOrio's theme was "God's Healing Love," and it was a wonderful experience to pray together as we did that day. My whole family felt that something special was happening. They did not realize just how special that something was until Father said, before he ended the service, that he had one more "word of knowledge." He called out that there was a woman wearing a black onyx ring with a diamond who was being healed of a blood disorder and arthritis. As he started to call this, my body began to shake uncontrollably and I felt a sensation of burning heat.

A year prior to the service, the doctor had told me that I had lupus. One of the symptoms of my illness was arthritis, along with extreme fatigue that required me to have ten hours of sleep at night and a rest period during the day. I also had skin rashes and loss of hair. Every four hours, around the clock, I had to take aspirin, and the doctor had forbidden me to go out in the sun.

I knew that I was the one being called by Father DiOrio that day in the service. Not only had I been hospitalized with severe arthritis that was associated with a blood disorder, but I was wearing a heart-shaped onyx ring with a diamond center. I just couldn't get out of my seat quick enough to claim this healing! As Father prayed with me, all at once I felt an amazing surge of energy rush through my body and I was slain in the Spirit. When I got up, Father said that Jesus had completely healed me and all of the lupus had gone out of my body. This indeed was my day! It was July 10, 1982.

More than a year has passed since I received my healing and I have never felt better in my life. My blood levels are normal and I have not had any signs of lupus. Neither have I had even a tinge of arthritis. I think of the times that I had to take Darvon and aspirin twelve to fourteen times a day to reduce the pain. Since that day at the service I have not needed either. My heart tingles every time that I think of how much Jesus loves me, to have taken all of that pain away. I realize now that He neither made me sick nor wanted me to suffer. He suffered for me, and all I had to do was to give my suffering to Him. It is as if my healing was only a prayer away.

Jesus truly is my Lord and Saviour! Not only did He heal me physically, but He touched me spiritually as well. In return for all that He has done for me, I have given myself to Him. He provides everything that I need and I don't worry any more, because I have learned to trust Him.

I also feel that I have become a better parent. I have been

able to guide my children spiritually now that I understand more about Jesus.

It is a pleasure to teach children in my first-grade CCD class that Jesus loves all of us regardless of who we are or what we do. To teach them their prayers and to tell Jesus that they love Him is a privilege.

When Jesus touched me to make me whole again, He offered me forgiveness. He gave me a second chance, a new life that belongs to Him. I believe that He proves His love by healing us. He pours out His blessings upon all who receive Him. Just believe and receive or doubt and do without.

PRAYER:
Dear Lord, one of the finest graces You can render to us, Your children, is that gift of trust. I seem to hear the mouth of the wise man saying, "Yes, trust in the Lord with all your heart, and never from His ways depart, and He will bless you all your days." How true are those thoughts from the Book of Proverbs! Lord, I know that they are true because I myself have become the beneficiary of that truth of trust in You. You heard my cry, You received my earnest prayer. Good St. Paul challenges us to think of our experience when, in his First Letter to the Corinthians 4:7, he stresses that we should name something we have received, and recognize it as God's gift. ". . . pray constantly; and for all things give thanks to God . . ." (1 Thessalonians 5:18).

Medelise Summa

A DISTANT HOPE

*. . . to give light to those who live
in darkness and the shadow of death. . . .*

Luke 1:79

Psychologists claim that whether depression be acute or chronic, it is accompanied by a paralyzing sense of helplessness. Some depressed persons have claimed that they felt powerless to alter the situation in which they found themselves. There seemed to be no alternatives to choose. All hope seemed at a distance. Such is the frailty of being human. And more so is the agony of that pain that comes upon the mind as well as that of the body and the spirit.

The following story tells about a married woman, mother of six children, who suffered severe depression. On occasion, the lady of this story took refuge in alcohol, which complicated her dire situation. But, regardless of how we humans may seek to escape from ourselves, our heavenly Father will eventually attempt to break through the defense mechanisms, the human blockades set up. His grace of love, calling each human person to Himself, is a constant reminder that all men and women, His children, are important. God Himself, loving the soul He created in His human beings, will slowly penetrate that blockade. With the Divine Providence of inner healing, God allows the accumulated hurts of a lifetime to be relived in the very heart and in the very wounds of God's Son, Jesus. In that very process, hope that was a stranger, hope that appeared distant, becomes the hope for a better and new tomorrow.

Eighteen years ago I was stricken with a severe depression after the birth of our sixth child. I had to be hospitalized for quite some time. With proper care, medication and much prayer, I slowly was able to get back and function at home. With many ups and downs, just too difficult for me to describe, I continued on in this fashion under the care of an excellent doctor.

At this time in my life, the doctor felt that I was a manic-depressive and immediately started me on lithium, along with other medication. Things seemed to level off for a while and I was much better, but far from well.

Socially I was a heavy drinker and enjoyed drinking. Suddenly the doctor saw a noticeable change in my behavior when I was drinking while taking lithium. Due to this behavior I was told to stop drinking entirely. I did not want to stop, nor did I want to listen. Needless to say, I suffered the most severe depression that I had ever experienced. No one thought that I would ever be well again. Those days were days of hell on wheels, and I was terrified beyond description.

Somehow I managed to call Father DiOrio's prayer line to ask for prayer. Within four days I experienced marked relief. This was in January of 1982. During the same week, I was miraculously able to secure a reservation for an upcoming retreat that Father was giving. I then felt reassured that I would be all right if only I could make it to that retreat.

When I finally arrived in Waltham, Father prayed with me and I had great faith that I would be just fine. From then until the present, I have not had a desire for alcohol, nor have I experienced any highs or lows. Presently my doctor is in awe. He cannot believe that I have been completely stable for a year!

Above all, I am most grateful to God for healing me through a most beautiful instrument of God who is loved dearly with a grateful heart.

PRAYER:
Dear, dear Father in heaven, how precious is Your loving

concern for us Your children! Darkness always seems to follow each day. But then again, light follows the darkness too. The light is so illuminating; it guides us on to better insight, to proper goals of living. But, dear Lord, the darkness is so frightening! Where can we find strength? To whom shall we go? Only to You, dear Lord. And I thank You for never having forgotten me. There are no secrets or problems or mysteries in Your total sight. Thank You for looking upon me in my darkness, in my pain, in my utter perplexity. Thank You for saving me from my inner slavery, from my resentment of everybody and everything around me: my loved ones, my friends, my neighbors. Thank You for saving me from self-pity, and above all from distrust and despair. All that I ask now, dear Lord, as You have touched me with your healing love, is that You give me Your continuous flow of grace when I am feeling nothing, when I think that my life has no plan. Let no darkness obscure my vision of You. Let Your guiding light be ever the rainbow beyond my tears.

Stephen Tabone

———

HOW CAN I DOUBT TO FIND THEE EVER?

I was pressed, pressed, about to fall,
but Yahweh came to my help;
Yahweh is my strength and my song,
he has been my savior.

Psalm 118

It is true that in the last analysis each person must stand alone. No matter how many people surround one, or how famous one may be, in the most significant moments of life a person will necessarily find himself alone. The real moment of a new birth springs forth from "an alone world," as in the very moment of death. Within these significant moments (from birth to death) there is the aloneness of the moments of tears, moments of struggle for improvement, moments of growth, moments of decision. There are times when a person is forced to be only with himself/herself. The following story inspires the reader. It speaks of a man who had Guillain-Barré syndrome. This illness is an acute, rapidly progressive disorder of the peripheral nerves. It is characterized by muscular weakness and mild sensory loss, which usually begins shortly after a banal infection. Symptoms begin peripherally, often in the fingers or toes, and progress inward. Although numbness, tingling, and other signs are common, there may be mild sensory loss and muscle tenderness, and muscular weakness predominates. The weakness often ascends from legs to arms and to the face. In severe cases, cranial nerve and trunk muscles may be involved and respiration may be impaired. The respiratory paralysis may be life-threatening. In Stephen's case, he was diagnosed as seriously ill with this disease. This particular illness, although it brought Stephen into a state of depression and dependency, causing him to enter within himself, experiencing "aloneness," nevertheless served a divine purpose. This state of aloneness caused Stephen to turn to the Lord in a deeper relationship of divine abandonment. This was the stepping-stone to his recovery. Step by step, moment by moment, Stephen is well on his way, resuming normal functioning.

It was Saturday morning. My wife, Marie, was making her usual telephone calls to our three daughters, who all reside in Florida, when we got our first indication of Stephen's illness. What first appeared to be a relatively simple backache turned out to be a strange-sounding malady.

It seemed like only yesterday when Angela and Stephen first met. They were both so young. Angela was all of fifteen and a half and Stephen was almost seventeen years old. One day our little girl came home from Plainedge High School, in Massapequa, New York, with the news that she had met a very nice boy, named Stephen. "All of the girls are after him, but he only wanted to be with me," she bubbled to her mother. We were sympathetic and understanding. Stephen's parents, however, looked on their dating as threatening, even though their get-togethers occasionally occurred in our home under the watchful eyes of Marie.

Stephen was the eldest of seven children. His parents raised their children in a loving and caring one-family home close to the school and church. It was not uncommon to find the pastor of Maria Regina Catholic Church visiting them and sharing in their evening meals. Then Sunday mornings found the whole family at church together.

Marie and I tried to allay Stephen's parents' fears over a cup of coffee one evening. "Besides," I said, "we may not be living here much longer. The Naval Training Device Center, in Port Washington, New York, where I am now employed, may be relocating to Florida." Despite this reassurance, they severely restricted Stephen's visiting and dating Angela. Even at this tender age, Stephen displayed an unusual determination, which surfaced in his always clean-shaven face. His shining black hair, combed neatly in place, appeared to glisten even more.

While they continued to see each other only on "special occasions," plans were being finalized for the Naval Training Device Center's inevitable move to Orlando in late 1965. We left Massapequa as soon as Laura, another daughter, graduated from high school. Stephen also graduated at this time.

Time and distance did little to diminish their love for each other; it only served to fuel Stephen's determination. And so Stephen, with a heavy heart, left home and arrived at our doorstep in Winter Park, Florida, timid and forlorn, but exuberant at seeing Angela once again. Although I chastised him, I could not turn him away. I helped him find a job, with the admonition to write and call his parents often.

Stephen enrolled for evening classes at the local college. Initially he could not afford a car, so he took the bus to work and walked to the college at night. Marie and I would drive over to Stephen's furnished room to pick him up for the weekends so that he could visit with Angela. All of this occurred at the height of the Vietnam War. Stephen would not wait to be drafted, so he enlisted and spent thirteen months in Korea, being discharged as a sergeant.

Just about a month after his return to the United States, on July 26, 1969, Stephen and Angela were married in St. Margaret Mary's Catholic Church, in Winter Park, Florida. Stephen's parents were indeed happy to witness the marriage ceremony of their firstborn.

In late October of 1982 Stephen was helping his two children to get dressed to go trick-or-treating on a quiet, tree-lined street in Jacksonville. Most of the neighbors were elderly and eagerly awaited the insistent ringing of their doorbells, to be startled by the adorable little children in their quaint costumes. The "little child" in Stephen was anxious to live the experience once again, and so he hastened them along.

"Stephen had to turn back with the children last night," exclaimed Angela. "His back was hurting him so badly that I put him to bed with some aspirin. I had to take the children to the rest of the neighbors."

It was not like Stephen to let Angela out in the night with the children. At thirty-four years of age, Stephen stood just under six feet; handsome, lean, muscular and gifted. He was equally adept at turning out a sensitive oil painting as fixing a cantankerous automobile. There was a time when he and Angela had driven to Massapequa, New York, to visit his parents in a 1965 Volkswagen Bug. No sooner had they arrived, on a cold, blustery day, than the car finally gave an exhausted shrug and would not budge any farther, as if to say, "I've had enough." Stephen and his brother took the engine apart, replaced the broken piston and put the entire engine together while blowing on their hands to keep warm. We dismissed the present incident from our minds until Thanksgiving Day.

Our eldest daughter, Laura, lives in Tallahassee, a tedious five-hour drive from our home, in Orlando. "This year," she said firmly, "we're having Thanksgiving at my house. I miss the family get-togethers that we used to have, especially our songfests." And before taking another breath, she stated, "I've already called Denise and Angela and everything is all set. You won't have to do any cooking, Mother."

We arrived at Laura's house early and awaited our children and grandchildren. Stephen, very slowly and apparently in much pain, struggled to get out of the car. It was then that we noticed that Angela had driven. Our grandchildren excitedly rushed to greet us after a long, three-hour drive confined to the back seat, with nothing to do. Angela looked tired and annoyed, but mustered up a cheerful smile as she carried home-baked goodies into the house. It was a pleasant day, but everything seemed to focus on Stephen. We shared his discomfort grudgingly, because we wanted a happy and memorable occasion. He was miserable and could not get comfortable no matter what he did, including hot baths and stretching out on the floor. Several visits to the chiropractor had done nothing for his disposition. The traction equipment that he had rented failed to provide relief, and his pain was persistent. All day a dismal mood prevailed, and even our singing failed to alleviate his pain. Only the pain-killers prescribed by his doctor and extremely hot baths for hours on end offered some relief.

It was early in December when Angela called to say that

Stephen was being admitted to St. Vincent's Hospital, in Jacksonville. A neurosurgeon suspected a slipped disc but wanted him in the hospital for further tests and possible surgery. The next day, I heard the words "CAT scan" and "possible tumor" over the telephone. Before my wife could stop me, I was in my car and headed for the hospital to be with my daughter and son-in-law.

The doctor was candid and to the point. "I am baffled! All of the tests are negative," he said. However, a noted neurologist who had been called in for consultation provided the dreadful diagnosis after examining Stephen at length. There was no question in his mind that Stephen had Guillain-Barré syndrome. Within two weeks he was to become paralyzed from his toes to his chest.

Contrary to one physician's advice, Stephen asked his other doctor to sign him out of the hospital on December 11 to be with his children, who were bewildered by his absence. It was the first time that he had been away from the children without reassuring them of his quick return. Besides, Stephen reasoned, there was nothing that the hospital could do for him other than bed rest and he could get that at home. He and Angela would work it out, but little did they realize what an ordeal they faced. I felt helpless and worried. Marie and I turned to the Lord and found solace in Psalm 55: "God, hear my prayer, do not hide from my petition. . . ." We prayed and asked others to pray with us, literally storming heaven with prayer. Everyone that we encountered promised to pray for Stephen. So we remained steadfast to the words of Jesus: "And everything you ask in prayer, believing, you shall receive" (Matthew 21:22).

Two weeks before Christmas, Angela told us that Stephen was much worse. Only with the aid of a walker was he able to take slow, halting steps and stand for a short period to shave himself. With much difficulty, he would literally slide into the tub for his bath. Gradually his legs would not hold him any longer. They simply collapsed from his weight, causing him to fall backward. On numerous occasions he was just spared serious injury.

"The children are so anxious to get the Christmas tree up,

Dad. Can you come and help me?" Angela pleaded over the phone.

"I'm on my way, honey," I replied. Marie was now used to the routine and everything was ready. The three-hour drive to Jacksonville gave me time to meditate and pray.

I found Stephen determined but desolate. "How could this happen to me?" he asked over and over again. The creeping paralysis was steadily inching up his body. To get around the house, he crawled on all fours. It was the only way for him to get from one place to another without being carried. I watched and choked back my tears.

Angela and I struggled with the fresh needles of a "real tree," and the children were delighted to see it standing upright. They helped to decorate the tree ever so carefully, with Stephen enjoying their squeals of delight. He even tolerated the random placement of ornaments, something that his nature would not normally have allowed. Everything had to be just so!

Almost every night, Angela was awakened by Stephen because the pain of being in one position became unbearable and he could not turn over. With great difficulty she would pull at his body until he was made a bit more comfortable. Interrupted sleep, night after night, began to affect them both; but they felt the infant Jesus understood their irritability. Meanwhile the children eagerly awaited Santa Claus, oblivious of everything else.

Stephen's disposition improved with the arrival of his parents and brother on December 20. But his condition worsened. He was now confined to a wheelchair, and the paralysis of his lower body was total. He would look at his toes and wonder why they would not respond. Not even a slight movement was possible. Prolonged periods of depression ensued.

The sun was shining brightly as the wheelchair was carefully threaded through the narrow confines of the Tabone kitchen. Some of the door moldings had to be removed to permit the wheelchair to reach the back door. Stephen was amazed at the wooden ramp his dad and brother erected. A broad smile crossed his face as the first rays of sunshine made contact with his body. He basked in the sunshine and fresh air, breathing deeply.

From the first week that Stephen was discharged from the hospital, a physical therapist had visited their home. Stephen's modest income and mounting medical expenses added to their miseries. Night after night they followed the therapist's routine, with Angela constantly encouraging Stephen to try to move his limbs or at least wiggle his toes as she helped him to undress.

One could not help but notice Stephen constantly clenching and unclenching his hands. We all knew that the paralysis threatened his respiratory system and silently prayed that it would not reach his lungs. If this were to happen, immediate hospitalization in a respirator would be needed to keep him alive. His strength was slowly ebbing from his fingers. With one hand he would position his fork onto the food and press the fork down into the food with the other hand. Cutting his fingernails was a monumental task. He finally gave up after trying to press the cutter unsuccessfully.

Shortly after Christmas, *The Florida Catholic* newspaper contained an article regarding Father DiOrio's scheduled visits to Gainesville, Saint Augustine and Jacksonville. At the same time, announcements were being read at the Catholic churches in these areas. Then we talked to friends about one of Father DiOrio's visits.

Jacksonville, Florida, was Father DiOrio's next stop. "We're going to get Stephen to Father DiOrio's service," my wife insisted, "and I don't care how many people are going to be there." I reassured her of my support. It was Stephen whom I was concerned about. How would he receive this news? What if he didn't want to go? What if he goes and nothing happens? I rationalized on and on.

Angela had different concerns. "Do you know that Stephen can't sit for more than two hours without discomfort? What about his medication? What about the bathroom? It's going to be difficult to get a parking space at that end of town. We may not even get into church, with all of those crowds."

Marie cast aside the concerns of both of us, and the words of the disciple Thomas came to me: "Unless I shall see in His hands the imprint of the nails, and put my finger into the place of the nails, and put my hand into His side, I will not believe" (John 20:25).

"Stephen, Mom wants you to attend Father DiOrio's service at Christ the King Church on Sunday. How do you feel about it?" I asked.

He looked at his emaciated body. There was no hesitation. "I want to go," he said.

"You know, Stephen," I replied, "there will be lots of people who may be disappointed. It's important for you to understand that." I quickly added, "But spiritual healing is much more important than physical healing."

"I know," he said. "I want to go!"

The one bathroom in the Tabone home was in constant use on Sunday morning, January 16. Christ the King Church was on the other side of town. Father DiOrio's service was scheduled for two o'clock, and judging from his other two appearances, we envisioned crowds of people already converging on that area. By eleven o'clock in the morning, Angela had Stephen in his wheelchair, dressed and full of expectation. A slick board had been previously tested to slide Stephen across so that we could get him from the wheelchair into the car and vice versa.

From the living room, I heard Marie speaking on the telephone as she obviously repeated with astonishment: "The church is already filled and closed? Even the Sacred Heart Chapel?" With a look of disappointment, she replaced the telephone in the cradle and turned to me and then to Stephen. "Do you still want to go, Stephen?" she asked.

"Yes" was his reply. He quickly added, "I don't care if we have to wait outside to see Father."

"Then, we'll let the Lord pave the way," said Marie.

Angela and I just looked at each other without comment. It was useless to make any. Determination and faith were written all over Stephen's and Marie's faces.

My first concern was realized as we approached the area where Christ the King Church is situated. Cars were everywhere! Parked in haphazard fashion as if abandoned, they occupied every available piece of real estate.

"Please, Lord," I muttered to myself, "help me to find a parking space."

As I slowly drove my car between the seemingly endless rows of automobiles, a space suddenly appeared. I smiled to myself and said, "Thank You, Lord."

We quickly slid Stephen, with the aid of our slick board, from the automobile to the wheelchair. Then we promptly headed in the direction of the church, with Marie and Angela trailing behind. The policeman was sympathetic and quick to remove the hastily erected barrier; he waved us toward the chapel. "There is absolutely no room left in the church," he remarked.

Sacred Heart Chapel is situated directly behind the church altar. As we steered Stephen into the chapel at twelve-thirty, the thought of waiting for the two-o'clock service to even begin began to occupy my thoughts. Stephen usually cannot tolerate more than two hours of continuous sitting in his chair. At home Angela would slide him onto the bed and roll him over like a sack of potatoes. He had lost thirty pounds; it was all muscle mass.

One quick look about the chapel shocked me back into reality. Wheelchairs of all descriptions were neatly lined up close to each other as if to make use of every available inch of space. There were children, pathetic sights of persons inhaling oxygen, worried mothers, young men and women, elderly ones clutching their canes and walkers. All had one thought: healing! Despite their apparent suffering, everyone turned toward Stephen being wheeled into the very last remaining space. Marie, Angela and I looked at each other and spoke not a word. The Lord was completely in charge. We had already witnessed two "miracles."

The singing had started, and from the television monitor installed in the chapel we were able to see Father DiOrio's entrance. The chapel became still. No one moved. All eyes were glued to the monitor. We could feel the intense, yet silent excitement. I looked toward Stephen from where I had positioned myself and wondered about his thoughts. "Please, Lord, touch him and all of Your children," I silently prayed.

It was not until five o'clock that Father DiOrio was directed to the chapel by one of his aides, having just returned from the courtyard surrounding the church. There were people everywhere! Stephen had now been sitting for almost six continuous hours, with Angela hovering over him with sips of water and pain pills. Father DiOrio was approaching the chapel, and I felt the overwhelming presence of the Holy Spirit. He went directly to the first wheelchair, occupied by a young paralyzed man who had recently returned from France and was brought to the service by his parents. After a few moments of prayer and meditation, Father DiOrio turned toward Stephen and spoke quietly to him. Angela looked on with tears falling gently down her face. This was the moment for which we had both longed and prayed.

"I feel a healing taking place," Father DiOrio said to Stephen. After anointing him and Angela with oil, he moved on to the next wheelchair.

I quickly withdrew Stephen's wheelchair and pushed him toward the door, for I was aware of his prolonged discomfort. We drove home hastily so as to free him from the monotony of the wheelchair. I sounded the horn just as I turned the corner toward his house, and a neighbor quickly responded. He lifted Stephen bodily from the car after unfolding the wheelchair from the trunk. In a matter of seconds, he had wheeled Stephen into the house and laid him on the living-room rug. Relief did not come instantly. It was not until much later; after another pain pill and some dinner.

"It'll be nice to feel the comfort of our bed," I said to Marie. "It's not too late. Let's drive home and leave them alone."

The phone rang unusually late on Monday evening. Our children had a custom of calling seconds after eleven o'clock to take advantage of the economical long-distance rates. It was almost eleven-thirty.

"Something must be up," I remarked as Marie reached for the phone by our bedside.

"Get on the other phone. Something wonderful had happened! Stephen wiggled his toes; a real noticeable wiggle," Angela said excitedly. In just one octave lower than Angela's voice, Stephen confirmed the miraculous event. His healing had started! Praise God!

And so it began. One call followed another, announcing small but significant improvements. In a matter of two short weeks, Stephen was able to get in and out of bed unaided. He was able to actually lift his legs off of the floor. The home therapist found little to do. Stephen was on his own. Strength was flowing throughout his body, and he exercised with renewed vigor. His life had changed; not only physically but, more important, spiritually.

In early March, Stephen felt well enough to visit us in Orlando. We were waiting outside of our home to greet him. Our grandchildren waved frantically when they spotted "Nana" and me in the driveway. I helped Angela to unfold the wheelchair, and Stephen proudly swung his legs out of the door, stood up, smiled broadly and sat down with ease. We covered him with hugs and kisses; the children could not fully understand our excitement.

As a family we attended the five o'clock Mass on Saturday evening at Saints Peter and Paul Church, full of gratitude and love for the Lord Jesus Christ. The seeds of faith that had been planted and nurtured by Stephen's parents when he was a young child had borne fruit. Stephen was healed! ". . . for truly I say to you, if you have faith as a mustard seed, you shall say to this mountain, move from here to there, and it shall move; and nothing shall be impossible to you" (Matthew 17:20).

Stephen's determination surfaced again when, on March 21, 1983, with the use of a walker he went back to work on a part-time basis as Chief of the Examination Support Staff for the Internal Revenue Service. On April 4, he advanced to canes, using them at the IRS office to steady his legs, which were still somewhat wobbly. His co-workers marveled at his rapid recovery, listening intently as he recalled the day that the Lord touched him. "It was a special time for us because we got to know each other again. And to know the Lord," Stephen said, "has changed my life."

PRAYER:
My Lord, Jesus, how can I thank You for the gift of faith that

*You granted me in those moments of experiencing "alone-
ness"? Lord, perhaps without this illness I would not have
had the time to stop and be with myself. There is so much
strength in being "alone," especially when in one's aloneness
one is able to be with You. And so I thank You for that period
in my life. Without it I could not have enriched my faith in
You. As I thank You, my Lord, I cannot help but think of the
thoughts of George Macdonald, who once said that a man is
perfect in faith only when he can come to God in the utter
death of his feelings and desires, without a glow or an aspi-
ration, with the weight of low thoughts, failures, neglects,
and wandering forgetfulness, and say to him, "Thou art my
refuge."*

George Tracy

MY COPILOT IS GOD

Claim me once more as Your Own, O Lord,
and have mercy on me.

Roman Breviary

Strange how God can use the ordinary events of each moment of each day to reawaken our lethargic, world-orientated lives to His ever quiet presence! Like the Apostles who followed Jesus, we at times forget that He is ever present in our bark of voyage. Perturbed and distracted by the events of life with all its struggles, with all our valiant forward marching we at times forget that once we were willing to walk and ride with the Lord. But somewhere along the line an unexpected event halts us to ask and to seek the meaning of the way. Interestingly enough, the answer always indicates that the presence of the Lord is quietly resting in the bark of our lives, waiting peacefully for our beckoning to Him. When we find Him, we call. So, "obediently," He arises to manifest his power over the forces of nature that have engulfed us. In the following narration, George Tracy speaks of the great renewal he received so unexpectedly. God was sitting with him in his own car one Sunday afternoon. George had forgotten about the presence of his unseen Guest, a Guest Who was to heal him. In that healing, George not only was blessed with bodily restoration but, through the power of the Spirit, was renewed according to the fruits of the Spirit.

It all began at a tollbooth on the Massachusetts Turnpike. I was paying my toll when I overheard the attendant say that

Father DiOrio was conducting a service. This was the moment that the Spirit chose to change my life.

I went to the service, which was being held at an outdoor shrine. It was July 19, 1981, and a warm day. The sick were everywhere. It was a sight to behold! They were gathered in wheelchairs and some were on stretchers. There were families together, and others alone. But somehow I knew there were no strangers.

I managed to get close as Mass began. Don't we all like a firsthand view? The sun had gone down and candles were lit in the hands of the sick. And I knew in my heart that such beauty was unique.

Since the mid-sixties I had been in severe pain from disintegrated cervical discs. My neck was only partially mobile, and so surgery was pending. I had already been through lower-back fusions, but my condition had progressively grown worse. Surgery offered only a minimal guarantee.

There, in Sturbridge, Father called me out of the crowd. Movement was affirmed and I was released from my pain. It had been fifteen years since I had been without pain.

Since childhood I had been a documented diabetic. Often it was difficult to create a balance. Then, one day, at a service that Father DiOrio conducted at Manhattan College, I was called forth from among seven thousand people. He identified me down to a maroon turtleneck sweater. That day it was diabetes from which the Lord freed me. Truly this was marvelous! But, just the night before, I had also been healed. God had given me a new outlook on life!

The following is a note from a physician who ordered a glucose tolerance test for George Tracy after he received his healing. Unlike those that had been done prior to his healing of diabetes, this test was entirely normal:

Mr. George Tracy has been treated for Diabetes with oral Diabinese for many years. After a service on April 3, 1982, at Manhattan College where he was named to be healed, a Glucose Tolerance Test on April 27, 1982, was entirely normal.

                                                        Dr. N.

PRAYER:

Dear Lord, You seem to show up in and at the most unexpected and unusual places. I never thought that the pain and anguish I have had both with my back and with diabetes would be healed in that Sunday-afternoon car trip. I rather am amusing myself as I think about that day and that incident of a car jamming through all that extraordinary traffic. Those cars were piled up for miles! And so I asked the man at the tollbooth what all this traffic was all about. He told me that some religious event was taking place. And so, being inquisitive by nature, I figured I would find out. And when I did, there You were, ready to invite me to Your healing session. And so it was I stopped and I attended, I prayed and I sang. When I went back to my car, I realized that I was healed. As I sat there in my car, I could not believe the reality of that day's events. I actually spoke out loud as if someone were in the car with me. And when I did, lo and behold, I felt I heard George Burns, in his movie Oh, God, *simply say, "It's me, George, let's praise God, and let's get moving." And so, now as I swim and run, and have a lot of fun, all I can say is "Thank You, God, for being there with me."*

Maria Trunfio

———

WHY DID GOD LET ME EXPERIENCE HODGKIN'S DISEASE?

*Unload your burden on to Yahweh,
and he will support you;
he will never permit
the virtuous to falter.*

                            Psalm 55:22

So very often people who become sick, and people who hear of some tragic illness affecting friends or relatives, point the finger of accusation at Almighty God. Somehow, all of us at sometime or other have blamed God for errancies, illnesses, catastrophes,—whatever brings no joy. We believe that God, supposedly being Almighty, should have all the power to avert all forms of harm, all forms of ugliness. Many of us would be surprised to realize that sickness, disease, catastrophes and all that is negative to sound living do not come from God. God is a Lord of life, of health. Illnesses and evil come from Satan, from original sin. Satan is the father and the founder of original evil; and we poor mortals suffer its consequences. But the healing power consists right in this fact: that we, united with God, can challenge the effects of original evil. In so doing, we expel the satanic forces from us. To hear the word of God proclaimed with authentic and real belief by him or her who teaches, preaches and prays, instills within the people a faith in Truth and in Spirit. Upon this, signs and wonders follow. In the case of Maria Trunfio, she, too, might just have asked the same question. Maybe she, too, looked for the answer in the fashion of humanistic responses. Nevertheless, God breaks through whatever condition of life, pain or suffering, and He speaks to us that there is healing through faith in the person of Jesus, Son of God, victory over all diseases in the rebuking of satanic forces, and loyal trust in adhering to the exhortation of Psalm 55:22:

Unload your burden on to Yahweh, and he will support you. . . ."

In September of 1980 I had a total hip replacement because of severe arthritis. It was then that I came to know the Lord. While on crutches for three months I spent a lot of time praying and growing in His love. But once I was walking on my own again, I spent less and less time in prayer. I tell you this because I want to share with everyone just how much our heavenly Father loves and forgives us. This brings us to February of 1981, about five months after my hip replacement. This is when I was diagnosed as having Hodgkin's disease, stage three.

My illness was frightening to me. At times I had heard that Hodgkin's disease was fatal, and I didn't know what to expect. I had a lump on my neck and shortness of breath. I had persistent back pain and distressing nausea, along with itching caused by a skin rash. But in some ways the treatment was worse than the illness. The doctor removed my spleen and gave me forty-seven radiation treatments. As before when I was ill, I turned to the Lord. I called out to Him in my need. He didn't ignore me because I had left Him. He had waited so that He could answer my prayer.

In August of 1981 my husband and I attended a healing service in Glens Falls, New York. It was the first time that I had seen Father DiOrio. As I waited for the service to start, I prayed that, through this priest, our Father in heaven would heal me. On leaving the service, I was not convinced that I had been healed. But I felt peace in my heart. I was ready to accept the Lord with whatever He had in store for me.

When I heard that Father DiOrio was coming to our city in November, I was upset that I would not be able to go. We would be away at that time, so I did not try to obtain a pass for the church services. Then a friend called and offered a ticket, so I did not decline.

I arrived two and a half hours before the service was to begin. This time I asked God for a sign that I could give to my husband to restore his faith. Just the Monday before, we had gone to the doctor. He had ordered a repeat blood test, as my liver test was off. So I prayed, but not for my own healing. I asked only that my poor husband have faith.

When Father DiOrio called out the healings, I listened intently. I heard him call endometriosis, arthritis, and then cancer of the lymph glands. I had all of these illnesses. But I did not want to take anyone else's healing. He continued to call and no one answered. Father said, "It's a woman and she wears something red." I knew then that it had to be me. Heat flowed through my body, and under my coat was a bright red sweater.

I went up to Father DiOrio shaking and thanking God for my sign. He prayed with me, and in truth I was not sure of being slain in the Spirit. I rather smiled as I thought of my husband. My new plastic hip was not paid for yet. Where would my husband be if I fell and cracked it? Father asked if I was afraid of Jesus. I answered, "I love Him!" Then I fell to the floor and rested in the Lord.

My next blood test was fine, and X rays showed that my chest was normal. Since then I have had many checkups. There is no trace of disease in my body. The doctor claims that with my attitude I would have been healed. Little does he know that, without Jesus, I would have had no attitude.

PRAYER:
Dear Lord,
My faith in You sustains me.
You comfort me in sorrow,
You hold me when I am afraid,
You put your hand upon my pain.

For those who do not know You,
I give you my suffering.

Use me *to tell the poor You love them.*
Use me *to tell the weary You will give them rest.*
Use me *to light the darkness of despair.*
Use me *to breathe a gentle word of peace.*

Use me *to reach the least of Your brethren with the* Good
   News *of God's love.*
THEN *will I truly share the joy of my faith in You with the*
   world.

THANK YOU, LORD.

Antoinette Worth

HOPE FOR A BETTER TOMORROW

Loudly I cry to Yahweh,
and he answers me from his holy mountain.

Psalm 3:4

God has made his promises. And He will fulfill them; but one necessarily must remain open to accepting His word. God definitely helps those who ask that those promises be made a reality. The power of faith places a human, finite mind into the infinite hands of the eternal God. Placing one's life in the power of divine faith allows a person to be loved and cared for by an everlasting loving Father. So, in the case of Antoinette Worth, such a process was experienced. Antoinette suffered with myasthenia gravis, an illness characterized by great muscular weakness as well as increasing fatigue. The cause is unknown. It occurs most frequently in women between the ages of twenty and fifty. The onset is gradual. The illness affects primarily the muscles of the neck and the face, with those of the trunk and the extremities following. The course of the illness is variable. Sometimes it is rapidly fatal due to respiratory failure. The story of Mrs. Worth is quite interesting, as she, with a strong faith in her God, reached the heart of a Healing God.

The first time that Father DiOrio prayed with me was on May 26, 1982. My sister-in-law, Cathy, was critically ill with lymphatic cancer, and she was the mother of five children. We took her to see Father DiOrio, and after we had Mass, my mother and sisters insisted that I also be blessed because of my neuromuscular disease and infertility. But with Cathy so very ill, my problems seemed insignificant. That was the beautiful day that I received a spiritual healing.

Eight years previously I had been diagnosed as having myasthenia gravis, a neuromuscular disease that is characterized by extreme muscular weakness and fatigue. In the beginning of my illness I experienced weakness in my eyes and facial muscles. Within six months the muscle involvement had spread to my legs, arms, hands and respiratory system. The severity of the symptoms varied from time to time. After undergoing surgery in 1976 I was put on drug therapy and required to take medication every three hours in order to function in a somewhat normal fashion. Eventually I adjusted to the disease and the limitations it put on my life.

I was finally given the "go ahead" to have children. However, unfortunately I developed several problems. They ranged from a tipped uterus, which had to be surgically corrected, to endometriosis, blocked Fallopian tubes and irregular ovulation.

After several years of extensive surgery and treatment, I found it increasingly difficult to handle my infertility. Having always loved children, I just expected to have several of my own. With each month that passed, I became more anxious and depressed. Every time someone would get pregnant I would ask God, "Why not me?" I just could not understand why God was not blessing my husband and me with children when we love each other and have so much love to share.

During that service in May I felt a renewed hope for Cathy. I knew that God had blessed her already, as she was still alive and with her babies, while receiving the best medical care available. We had family and friends all over the world praying for her, and God had heard our prayers. I felt spiritually stronger, with a renewed faith, hope and love, and just knew that God would continue to help her.

I returned home that day with a refreshed outlook on my life and faith. Fortunately I had been brought up in a fine Catholic family and had received a good education through twelve years of parochial schools. But through a combination of both laziness and being unhappy with my parish, I had stopped going to weekly services. Father's sermon really hit home that day, and I decided to find a parish that I could feel close to God in. I did just that, and now, with every service, my religion and life have taken on new meaning.

The Blessed Mother has always been very dear to me and now I feel her increased presence and support. The peaceful yet exhilarated feeling that I have is very hard to explain. My whole life has changed. Although my schedule is still as busy and confusing as ever, my personality does not reflect it. I don't feel rushed as I hurry around every day. There is within me an ever-present tranquillity.

I also feel that the "Why God" questions have been answered. All of these things have happened in my life so that I would come to "know Jesus more clearly, love Him more dearly and follow Him more nearly." My spiritual life has been enriched and renewed and so has the faith of my family and friends.

On July 10 my family returned to Worcester. It was an incredibly moving experience. There were so many people there, all for different reasons but with one thing in common: it was nothing else but their faith in God.

I have been fortunate to be blessed with a very special peace that comes with the realization of God's presence in my life. But my heart was broken for all the gravely ill people at that service. All that I could do was to ask Jesus to let those people, especially the parents of the sick children, receive God's healing love. I felt their anguish and could not help but cry for them. I felt such compassion and love for people that I did not even know, and wanted them to receive the incredible peace that I had. Actually, I just knew that if they had the peace of Jesus' love, then they could handle what this earthly life had in store for them.

Jesus blessed me again that day and I was healed of myasthenia gravis. When the service was over I realized that I had not taken any medication in over four and a half hours and felt fine. Previously, if I had taken my medication ten minutes late I would have felt the effects of the disease.

The day after the service, my husband and I went for a two-mile walk, a task that for years had been impossible. The following morning I attended Mass and found that I was able to kneel for the first time in eight years. Each day, I continue to surprise myself by doing things that I had been incapable of even with medication. I have since been tested for myasthenia gravis and there is no apparent evidence of the disease.

Not only had I become physically stronger, but I had an inner energy that was exhilarating. No matter how hard I worked, I had a prayer in my heart. I knew that if it was God's will for me to have children then I would be blessed with them. If it was not to be, He would guide me and I would continue to find strength in His love. I had developed a better life of peace, faith and prayer.

In October, following another month of daily medication, injections and special procedures to help me to conceive, I decided that I just could not do it anymore. If it was in God's plan for me to have children, then I would have them, whether my tubes were blocked or my ovulation was irregular. I left it completely in His hands, and for the first time in many years I was not possessed by the daily routine of preparing to conceive. I was peaceful and knew that God would either lead me to adopt or bless me with a child.

My faith in God has transformed my life. My inner self is serene, and that is such a great blessing. I take each day as it comes and know that everything happens for a reason, even if it does not appear clear at that moment.

The night before Christmas Eve 1982, my prayers were answered. I found out that I was carrying the long-awaited child of my dreams! Jesus had not only blessed me, but He had done so at such a special time of the year. As I reflect on the events of this past year, I realize that I have been truly blessed.

PRAYER:
Faith . . . hope . . . love are tremendous virtues, O Lord. But in my case, I must say that faith brought me to the realization that Your love was that which I hoped for. With all three, You granted me the gift of healing. I thank You with all my being. Lord Jesus, in Your earthly life you performed many miracles of healing and yet You suffered so much for

our salvation. This mystery of health and suffering seems a paradox. But You, dear Lord, indicated by Your own word that the paradox is solved by living faith. *Lord, please continue to fill me with that faith. My faith in you, dear Master, was a seed faith planted in me by someone You chose along the days of my life. And because of that person, I was able to turn to You with a living faith, a faith that has granted me "a new chance at life." Lord, may this, my witnessing narration, also serve as a "seed-planting" for another needy human soul.*

CONCLUSION

A THOUGHT . . .

You have come to the end of this journey of personal lives, whose personal sorrows were turned into moments of new joy as God was allowed to take over. I personally thank you for taking this voyage into the lives of other human beings, persons who come from all walks of life. Yet, regardless of background and status, all of us must conclude that none of us are strangers to the palpitation of human experience.

This book of experiences of healing had been requested by a host of people who had read a few cited cases in my second book, published by Doubleday, *Called to Heal.* Those stories, which seem to have been so enriching and encouraging, became the occasion for another series of varied case studies. The present book, moreover, has been prepared for the general audience, for those who serve the sick, and for victims stricken with various forms of disease and illness.

It is hoped that these experiences of healing, related in honesty and in objectivity, will have been read and will be shared with discretion. The true stories narrated are precious realities to people who were sick, even in some instances unto the point of fatality. To these people, blessed with new, enriching life, flowing directly from the abundance of God, such realities are *precious values of truth.* It is my concluding wish that these persons who have willingly opened the secrets of their lives, of their union with God and of their relationship with others may continue to be for you an inspiring instrument of healing and spiritual renewal.

. . . AND A PRAYER FOR HEALING

Lord, You have told us to ask and we will receive, to seek and we will find, to knock and You will open the door to us.

I trust in Your love for me and in the healing power of Your compassion. I praise You and thank You for the mercy You have shown to me.

Lord, I am sorry for all my sins. I ask for Your help in renouncing the sinful patterns of my life. I accept with all my heart Your forgiving love.

And I ask for the grace to be aware of the disorders that exist within myself. Let me not offend You by my weak human nature or by my impatience, resentment or neglect of the people who are a part of my life. Rather, teach me the gift of understanding and the ability to forgive, just as You continue to forgive me.

I seek Your strength and Your peace so that I may become Your instrument in sharing those gifts with others.

Guide me in my prayer that I might know what needs to be healed and how to ask You for that healing.

It is You, Lord, Whom I seek. Please enter the door of my heart and fill me with the presence of Your Spirit now and forever.

I thank You, Lord, for doing this.

Amen.

FATHER RALPH A. DiORIO, a fifty-three-year-old diocesan priest in Worcester, Massachusetts, was born in Providence, Rhode Island, on July 19, 1930. At the age of fourteen, he entered Sacred Heart Seminary, in Melrose Park, Illinois, and was ordained there on June 1, 1957.

During his twenty-six years as a priest, his ministry has taken many varying turns. He has earned degrees in psychology, spiritual theology and social work and speaks six languages. He has held pastoral offices, engaged in mission and retreat works and directed youth ministries, radio and multiple-communication enterprises.

Eight years ago, commencing February 20, 1976, Father Ralph consented to accept charismatic involvement, and on May 9, 1976, he was blessed as a channel of God's healing powers and since has given full time to Christian renewal through the healing ministry.

Father DiOrio looks back on the unfolding of his life now and understands why God allowed him to be involved in so many aspects of ministry. It was all part of the process of growth and preparation when God would ask the complete surrender of self and then transform that gift into a charism to flow out automatically as a second nature.

Father DiOrio's healing powers were manifested on May 9, 1976 (Mother's Day), as he participated in a parish prayer meeting. He wrote a petition, as did others in the congregation, and asked Jesus "to grant me a whole new life in the priesthood, in that which is like a second nature to me, a healing ministry for the whole world, not just one little group."

Minutes later he found himself being brought to the altar to preach a sermon on the Mother of God and the Holy Spirit. Before the end of that meeting, Father DiOrio was called on to pray over several people with afflictions. A man with internal bleeding was relieved of pain and healed. A young woman plagued with mental problems experienced a trance and then claimed peace and healing. A young boy's paralyzed legs became movable, and numbers were slain in the Spirit as he blessed them.

God was "breaking me out" in three separate kinds of healings that day, Father DiOrio related: physical, spiritual and psychological. He found himself "fighting the Lord" at first and later broke down crying, saying, "God, this is real, isn't it?" And asking, "Why me?"

Father DiOrio does not let people believe that the gift he has been given is for his personal glory. "The gift is for God's people so that God may touch them and bring them to Himself. He has to pass His invisible life and grace to people through a channel that is visible."

The channels are many, Father says, and he declares that each person is uniquely endowed and can be used by God to make Himself known. "We just have to be ready and open to the power of His Spirit," he concludes.

While we may admire the gifts in others, Father DiOrio advises, "We should get to know ourselves, who we are, what we are, what gifts we have, and ask God to bless these natural gifts that we may give them back to Him to become a charism."